Collecting Silver

Collecting Silver

by
Elizabeth de Castres

Published by
Bishopsgate Press Ltd.,
37 Union Street, London. SE1 1SE

For Gordon and Tim

British Library Cataloguing in Publication Data

De Castres, Elizabeth
  Collecting silver.
  1. Silverwork—Collectors and collecting
  I. Title
739.2′23   NK7230

ISBN 0-900873-71-X

All enquiries and requests relevant to this title should be sent to the publisher, Bishopsgate Press Ltd., 37 Union Street, London, SE1 1SE.

Printed by Whitstable Litho Ltd.,
Millstrood Road, Whitstable, Kent.

Contents

Acknowledgments

The author gratefully acknowledges the help of all those who have assisted in the production of this book including the Joint Committee of The Assay Offices of Great Britain, the Birmingham Assay Office, the Worshipful Company of Goldsmiths, Asprey & Company, Christie's, J. H. Bourdon-Smith Ltd., Garrard and Company Ltd., Phillips, S. J. Shrubsole Ltd., Sotheby and Company, Spink and Son Ltd., the Victoria and Albert Museum.

Introduction

The history of silver is a long and fascinating one, stretching way back into antiquity. Silver has always been cherished, not only for its value as a precious metal, but also for its great beauty.

The historical aspect might seem remote to the ordinary collector of small and, perhaps, sometimes comparatively unimportant pieces. But this should not be so. The intriguing story of silver is related to practically every artefact in the home today, whatever this is from a simple spoon to a teapot. Silver was used for tableware long before such wares were produced in a satisfactory form of ceramics. In fact, when early English potters first began to produce wares they were careful to follow the shapes and designs already established by the silversmith.

Some people might argue that silver has out-priced itself. This is not always the case. There are many pleasing objects still to be collected by those who love this unique metal. These are readily available at prices which most people can afford. I am not, of course, talking about rare, esoteric objects, or singular collectors' items. I refer to more general pieces and those made towards the end of the Victorian era, early Edwardian items and even later. All are gradually increasing in value and, quite apart from the pleasure they bring, may prove to be a good investment providing a sensible price is paid. Knowledge can help here, which is where this book should be of assistance.

Apart from its beauty and value, silver has a further advantage. It is durable. Whereas a piece of china or glass is easily and irrevocably broken, a piece of sterling, hallmarked silver is always a piece of silver, even when dropped and perhaps dented, for you still have the value of the metal at least, and, depending on how serious the damage, it is always possible that you can have the piece satisfactorily repaired.

In addition to hallmarked silver, there are two other fields of 'silver' for collectors to consider. There is Sheffield plate, which was an eighteenth century innovation, and electro-plate, which was introduced in the nineteenth century and which is still being produced in large quantities today.

Good Sheffield plate has become expensive over the years, but, since a multifarious range of objects was made in it, there is always the chance of finding something at a realistic price, and, with this thought in mind, there is a chapter on Sheffield plate which will guide all those who are interested.

Electro-plate is the less collected of all three. At one time it was not collected at all. However, nowadays nineteenth century electro-plate and certain pieces made at the beginning of this century are ascending the price ladder and, since early electro-plate is not without charm and, in some cases, merit, it provides scope for collecting. The chapter on electro-plate will give basic guidelines and help to date certain objects.

All collectors should attempt to acquaint themselves with basic methods of manufacture, style and decoration, related to specific periods. Once they become familiar with these, they are in a far safer position to judge the authenticity of a piece. Although hallmarks are a fine guide when it comes to dating a piece, they should never be regarded as the ultimate proof of authenticity. As the relevant chapter reveals, frauds are not uncommon, and, while the hallmarks themselves might be correct, they may have originated on an earlier piece and been cunningly transferred. However, there are ways and means of detecting such skulduggery and these are discussed in the chapters on hallmarks and pitfalls.

Whatever the collector decides to pursue, he can be assured that a great deal of pleasure, many varied surprises and moments of exultation await him. To ensure a maximum of the latter, he would be wise to arm himself with the basic knowledge on these pages, and, thus equipped, carry on with renewed vigour the always pleasurable and often addictive pastime of collecting.

Elizabeth de Castres

CHAPTER 1

Silver and Its Beginnings

Long before small items of domestic silver began to filter into the home, silver was used for ecclesiastical purposes. This beautiful metal was a natural choice for Christians to use, not only for their vessels, but also for Church ornaments and embellishments. Moreover, the craftsmanship of these early pieces befitted the metal and was generally very fine.

As early as the eighth and ninth centuries, the reputation of Anglo-Saxon goldsmiths (goldsmith is used in its generic sense) was so highly regarded that numerous papal orders for English plate have been found documented, as have been costly gifts of plate from English monarchs to Rome as well as to religious orders in Britain.

It has been suggested that the fine work of the Anglo-Saxon goldsmith could be the result of the influence of two important historical figures, Alfred the Great (849–901) and a simple monk called Dunstan (924–88). Alfred improved the standards of craftsmen by an injection into Britain of skilled foreign workers who raised the standard generally and imparted new ideas of style and technique.

Dunstan, who later became Archbishop of Canterbury, with all the influence of this august position, was much interested in the craft of the goldsmith, and for a personal reason. Monks combined a craft with their religious devotions and Dunstan had worked as a goldsmith. Not only had he produced chalices, crosses and censers for his own abbey, but he had also worked on secular plate. His knowledge and experience was broad, therefore, and it was appropriate that he later occupied a singular place in the history of the goldsmiths of Britain. Dunstan was canonized and later made the patron, protector and founder of the goldsmiths of London and all England. Sadly, nothing produced by St. Dunstan remains today, but a thirteenth century royal inventory catalogues "a gold ring with a sapphire of the workmanship of St. Dunstan". His effigy which was of silver gilt and set with gems, long graced the hall of the London goldsmiths, and certain items of their corporate plate also incorporated his likeness. When a date letter was added to the London hallmarks in 1478, this was changed annually on May 19, which is St. Dunstan's Day.

Little very early silver remains as evidence of the high calibre of work by these ancient craftsmen. Various reasons for this include the fact that a great deal of the plate which was produced during the Dark Ages, particularly ecclesiastical pieces, found its way into the hands of the Norman conquerors, either to meet their demands or to procure their favour. Still more was later given by the Churches towards the ransom of Richard I, and in 1338 Edward III borrowed a

9

vast amount from abbeys and cathedrals, saying that he would replace the vessels that were melted down. Since melted-down silver and gold were in constant demand, it is easy to see why so little of it remains.

However, although there is a scarcity of early pieces, there are certain items of medieval domestic plate which are still here to delight us. These include the most important piece of all for the table – the standing salt. This was magnificent and splendid, but with only a comparatively small container for the precious salt. Books dealing with the subject of etiquette in the fifteenth and early sixteenth centuries reveal just how important the standing salt was – the position in which it was placed at table relating to title and rank of the diners. This impressive, and generally beautifully worked object, belonged, of course, to the age of the lord of the manor. Thus only the wealthiest of establishments would possess one. The principal standing salt would be placed to the right of the head of the house, the second at the lower end of the table, and the remainder on the other tables in the large, baronial hall, where all sat down to eat in those far off days before a separate dining room came into being.

An inventory of the plate of Edward III, taken in the fourteenth century, listed several hundred salts of varying types. Sir John Fastolf had eight large salts and a single one of five ounces, and the Earl of Oxford possessed sixteen large and four small salts. Medieval inventories and wills describe salts of intriguing shapes and decoration. Animals were popular and included dogs, elephants, dragons and lions. The Monkey Salt (c.1500) at New College, Oxford, has a decorated, circular pedestal, supported by 'feet' in the shape of wild men seated on cushions. Surmounting the pedestal is a further, larger cushion upon which is a very realistic figure of a chimpanzee. The gilt-mounted crystal bowl of the salt is balanced adroitly upon his head.

The Huntsman (giant) salt, c.1470 of All Souls College, Oxford, is of parcel-gilt and rock crystal, the hunter having painted hands and feet. He stands on a circular 'cushion' pedestal with miniature hounds around his feet and balances the circular receptacle for salt upon his majestic head.

Standing salts of varying shapes and dimensions followed until they became more or less obsolete by the time of the Restoration. The standing salt's position of social importance was then no longer in evidence because members of a household had long ceased to eat together in a large hall, and, while the standing salt might still appear at table. its original significance had certainly dwindled.

Thus the predecessor of the salt cellar as we know it came into being. Diners now took their salt from robust, sturdy little trencher salts. They were basic containers, variously shaped including circular, triangular, octagonal and quatrefoil. No definite English trencher salt prior to the seventeenth century appears to be known. One of the earliest is dated 1603 and is a simple, circular object. Samuel Pepys paid £6.14.6d for 'a dozen of silver salts' in 1665, and a set of twelve quatrefoil trencher salts, bearing the London hallmarks for 1662 were once the property of the Painter-Stainers' Company. Sets are rarely found, although a set of six is known, hallmarked for 1667. They are simple, circular little vessels, bearing the emblem of the family, the container for the salt, as was usual,

1. An unusual pair of electro-plated Victorian salts, cast, with raised oval bases designed in the form of sea waves, upon which rest finely modelled stylized dolphins supporting ammonite shells, c.1860. Centre: a Victorian child's silver-gilt mug by Hunt & Roskell, 1846. (Phillips)

being extremely shallow. These unpretentious pieces continued for many years. They were the forerunners of all the elegant shapes and designs which were to follow in the eighteenth century and later, and which we use on our tables to this day. They are fully discussed in the chapter on silver for the table.

In common with other medieval silver, very few spoons have survived. Certain examples of early spoons have been discovered, but they have been difficult to date specifically. A small spoon, the Warwick spoon, which it is thought was originally intended to be used with an incense boat, has been dated at approximately 1150–1350, but it was not until the fourteenth century that spoons began to find their way, in rare numbers, into the domestic scene. They did not much resemble the spoon we use today, however, for their true purpose was to spoon food into the mouth, and for this they were crudely and appropriately shaped. They were highly prized. The will of Edith Palmer, c.1305, talks of thirteen silver spoons marked with a star. Another, made at approximately the middle of the fourteenth century by John de Holegh, bequeathed twelve silver

2.   Left: St. Andrew apostle spoon, London, 1641; right: slipped-in-the-stalk spoon, London, 1641. (J. H. Bourdon-Smith Ltd.)

spoons; while a further, c.1361 signed by John Botiller, a draper, bequeathed to Isabella, his wife, twelve 'best spoons' with gilt acorns.

Approximately a century later, King Edward VI had in his possession a fine selection of spoons, some of which were New Year presents to the sovereign, which shows that a gold or silver spoon was a coveted status symbol, especially bearing in mind that the donor usually expected a present in return of a little more value than his own. (The custom of New Year gifts by the nobility to the sovereign was an important one, the value of the gift relating to the rank of the donor. It continued until about 1680).

Very gradually then the silver spoon became more general, first in the palaces of the sovereign and royal family, then in the fine houses of the nobility and wealthy land owners, until eventually finding a revered place in the homes of others with the means to purchase it. Extant examples of medieval spoons, although basic, have an individual charm of their own. Their knop finials are all important. Approximately 200 years were to pass before, at the beginning of the eighteenth century, the spoon began to emerge gradually as the graceful utensil, in its varying sizes, which we now use. (See Chapter 4)

Medieval plate, therefore, although appearing distant was, in some cases, the original 'ancestor' of many ubiquitous modern objects. It included handsome standing cups, mazers, drinking horns, beakers and ewers and basins.

Following the accession of Henry VIII to the throne the use of silver expanded rapidly. Silver was becoming more plentiful. Production in the silver mines of Germany and Central Europe saw big increases by the beginning of the sixteenth century, and later both gold and silver began to be imported from Spanish America in growing quantities. The increases in the availability of bullion resulted in a proportionate fall in its cost. The nobility and wealthy exploited the situation. Influenced by Henry VIII they spent lavishly and invested enormous amounts in vast quantities of silver, silver-gilt, gold and jewels. Cardinal Wolsey set a precedent and amassed so much that his collection was said to be as extensive as that of Henry VIII, with gold and silver dishes enough to fill thirty wagons. Thus the amount of extant plate made from the accession of Henry VIII in 1509 until the death of Elizabeth I in 1603 exceeds greatly that from the Middle Ages. Sadly, even this is only a small example of the enormous amount which was produced in such magnificence and beauty. Various reasons account for this, but the most important was the destruction of practically all the plate owned by the Church and its related foundations, both domestic and ecclesiastical, during the suppression of the monasteries and the Reformation. Other factors would have included those of economics and fashion.

The type of silver objects made during the sixteenth century, in addition to those already mentioned, included a new drum-shaped vessel, the tankard. This name eventually replaced the old, prosaic word, 'can', and denoted a drinking vessel with a hinged cover, thumbpiece and scrolled handle, generally reckoned to be of German or Scandinavian origin. One of the earliest known, entirely of silver, is dated 1556, and it is of an older, pear-shaped variety, without a lid. Only about fifteen examples of this type are known. From approximately 1570 metal tankards became more general, and they have continued with varying changes in style to the present day. Handsome Elizabethan tankards might be exquisitely decorated with flower and foliate patterns, and were also sometimes gilded, which added to their splendour.

Standing dishes upon a stem – sometimes referred to as a tazza – were another sixteenth century introduction. They were probably used to hold fruit or other food. In the centre of the shallow bowl was usually some form of embossed decoration, and round it would be further ornament.

Silver candlesticks were still very rare. A candlestick in the royal inventory of 1532 had a chain and snuffers engraved with H and K, a rose and a pomegranate. The advertisement for the state lottery held in 1567 illustrated among its prizes, a silver candlestick with sockets, short stems, wide grease pans and spreading base. This is believed to be the first mention of socket candlesticks made of silver, although Henry VIII is known to have possessed four made of gold, enamelled in red and decorated with his monogram. One of the earliest English silver candlesticks, made during the reign of Elizabeth I includes rock-crystal. It is a two-light example and is called the Sanford Candlestick, c.1580. The stem is gilt, decorated with eagles and satyrs supporting a crystal cross bar, to each end of which is attached a socket.

After the Restoration in 1660 the production of silver entered a new and prolific phase. Increasing prosperity among the nobility and wealthy resulted in a craving for luxury which manifested itself in a growing and unprecedented demand for English domestic silver. In addition, it was also necessary to replace the secular and ecclesiastical pieces which had been melted down during the Civil War. Most of the silver was made in London, which retained its fine reputation for the standard and expertise of its goldsmiths.

The royal family led the way, and in the palaces of ensuing sovereigns was installed a fortune in costly plate. Its beauty and opulence was emulated in every detail by the nobility, who in their turn were copied by the wealthy, and so on down the social strata, right through to the taverners. The use by taverners of silver tankards, basins, cups and bowls resulted in an outburst of robberies and an Act was passed which forbade them to expose in public all wrought or manufactured plate, except spoons.

Quite apart from smaller items of domestic silver which were now being used more commonly, the demand was also for certain pieces of such enormity that their existence is hard to believe. Among these was the gigantic vessel produced for the serving of wine which made its appearance at this time, namely the wine cistern. Sometimes the size of a small bath, its purpose was to hold the bottles of wine at banquets or similar functions. A cistern made for the Duke of Rutland in 1681, measured four feet in length and eighteen inches in height. Its weight was 3,000 ounces. In the Hermitage, Leningrad, can be found the largest of all, made by Charles Kandler (London) in 1734, which measures 5½ feet long. The weight is 8,000 ounces.

Other large, ostentatious pieces included silver furniture, which presented an awesome sight in all its magnificence. In the collection of the Queen is a table

3. A tazza with gadrooning around the surface and foot, c.1703.

which was presented to William III by the Corporation of London, c.1690. Accompanying it is a looking glass, 7 feet 6 inches in height. There are as well two complementing candlesticks. According to the inventory of the royal plate made in 1721, this suite of furniture weighed 7,306 ounces, the enormous weight being due to the fact that, instead of being constructed of a sheet of silver upon a wood frame, it was mostly made of solid silver.

Of more significance to most of us was a somewhat smaller object which was introduced towards the end of the seventeenth century. It was necessitated by the appearance of a beverage which has since become a vital part of the Englishman's daily life, namely a good cup of tea. A tea advertisement which appeared in the London Gazette in 1658, and which is thought to be the earliest reference to tea, reads: "That Excellent, and by all Physitians approved, China Drink, called by the Chineans, Tcha, by other Nations Tay, alias Tee, is sold at the Sultaness-head,

16

a Cophee-house in Sweetings Rents by the Royal Exchange, London". Samuel Pepys wrote of his first cup of tea in his diary two years later.

The earliest known English silver teapot (c.1670) can be seen at the Victoria and Albert Museum. It tends to look like a coffee pot, with a tall, cylinder-shaped body, tapering sides and a conical cover, topped by a small baluster finial. The handle, which is at right angles to the spout is partly covered in leather. An early coffee pot, made in 1681, is also in the collection of the Victoria and Albert Museum. Coffee was first introduced into England as early as 1637. Tea cups and saucers were not generally made in silver, although some were produced. The University of Bath has a rare fluted cup and saucer in its possession.

At the turn of the eighteenth century, English domestic silver was beginning, therefore, to embrace a growing number of the items used in modern homes. By the end of the eighteenth century the picture was complete. The diversity and range of objects made by the eighteenth-century silversmith included knives, forks, tea, dessert, table and caddy spoons, fish servers, ladles, sugar tongs, asparagus tongs, mustard pots, sauceboats, cake and fruit baskets, inkstands, needlework accessories, salvers, shaving basins, skewers, wine labels, vinaigrettes, nutmeg graters, patchboxes and snuff boxes, to name but a few.

The nineteenth century saw further additions. The field is wide, therefore, and is full of intriguing historical continuity which is what makes collecting such a fascinating way in which to spend one's moments of leisure.

4. *Facing Page: The earliest-known English silver teapot, 1670. (Victoria and Albert Museum)*

CHAPTER 2

Changing Styles and Techniques

Small collectable pieces of silver generally echoed the styles and techniques of larger objects, both secular and domestic. Thus an early nutmeg grater made c.1680 might be primitively hand engraved with a floral design or *chinoiseries* in the manner of more important pieces, even though the decoration might not have been accomplished with the same finesse. Similarly, nutmeg graters made during the nineteenth century, as with larger items, would be more heavily decorated in the style of the period, and commonly by mechanical means.

Needlecases, vinaigrettes and many other objects which were produced during the later years of the eighteenth century and early years of the nineteenth century were often decorated with bright-cutting, and because of this can be dated at that time, since it was then that this type of engraving was prevalent.

Thus, once a collector has assimilated a working knowledge of the change in styles and techniques through the centuries – and there were not so very many – it can be safely said that he stands a good chance of not falling prey to the more silken tongued dealer who may tend to date a piece unscrupulously.

When the eighteenth century arrived, decoration and techniques were in their infancy. The current style, known as 'Queen Anne', was dominant from about 1705 until approximately 1720. Its main characteristic was its simplicity. There was much charm in these early eighteenth century pieces with their scarcity of ornament. They had a satisfying air of substance. Their main artistic claim was in their carefully designed proportions which, together with their high degree of craftsmanship, makes them highly prized today. Prominent among English silversmiths of the period were, among others, Anthony Nelme and Benjamin Pyne.

However, English silversmiths were not the only craftsmen working in London at the time who were producing work of a high calibre. An important historical event of the previous century had a far-reaching effect on English silver, and this began to manifest itself now. The Revocation of the Edict of Nantes in 1685 meant that Huguenot craftsmen emigrated to other countries, including England. Many silversmiths settled in London, to the chagrin of English silversmiths, especially as the work of the Huguenots was superb and their skill enviable.

They brought with them different techniques and ideas which were a strong competition, and it was not long before they were being patronised by the wealthy who appreciated and could afford their products. By around 1700 the influence of the French silversmiths was recognisable and it became more so with the passing of the decade, so that by about 1720 it had made firm roots. Their style, like their work, was distinctive. Although decorative it was never over-stated. It featured, in general, ornament cast in high relief with heavy mouldings, perhaps gadrooned or fluted, with beautiful cut-card work (discussed under techniques later in this chapter). Small wonder then, that this ornate, distinguished work shone out against the simple, undecorated wares in which the London silversmith specialised. Important among early Huguenot silversmiths were David Willaume the elder and Pierre Platel the elder who came to London around 1687. In 1705, the most famous of them all, Paul de Lamerie, was apprenticed to Pierre Platel and seven years later punched his own mark for the first time, beginning a dazzling career which was to continue until 1751.

An inevitable integration of the two styles, Huguenot and London, gradually followed until they were both swallowed by the growing fashion for rococo. The rococo style was one of fantasy and imagination. Attributed, among others to Juste Aurele Meissonnier (1695–1750), who was among those seeking to break away from the heavy symmetry of the baroque, it was based upon asymmetrical patterns and C-. and S-scrolls, with rock and shell motifs. The French word for rock-work, *rocaille* gave birth to the word rococo. The style lent itself perfectly to decoration for all types of silver since it could be developed to whatever degree of embellishment was required. Thus it was as suitable for Church vessels as it was for secular or domestic pieces. Paul de Lamerie and Charles and Frederick Kandler were the most adventurous leaders of the rococo style in England during the early thirties, and they were responsible for pieces of astonishing fantasy and beauty.

Typical of the extravaganza of the period is a tea kettle and stand by Charles Kandler which incorporates practically every characteristic of ornate rococo. The kettle and tripod are encrusted with mythical characters from the sea against a background of marine life. Each foot of the tripod is cast as a triton, its body is heavily embossed with Neptune, followers and attendants. The spout is a demi-triton blowing a conch, while the finial is a boy, and the two arms of its swing-handle are mermaids.

Despite the fact that rococo dominated the fashion of the day, there were as well quite plain pieces of silver produced at the same time. The simple pieces were in demand by those, who, although wealthy enough to buy silver, could not afford the extra cost of the very ornate rococo, or, perhaps did not care for it. Certain examples of rococo tended to be less exaggerated with chased flowers, foliage, shells, scrolls and sometimes incorporating oriental or classical figures.

Thus the rococo fashion rollicked through approximately three decades of the eighteenth century, and it must have appeared to most devotees that it would continue to do so. But this was not to be the case, for it was confronted by another vogue which was such a success that it was responsible for the very quick demise of the rococo style, replacing it in popularity practically before the provincial silversmith had probably realised that it was on the wane. The new fashion was the neo-classical style which established itself by the 1770's, having begun to make inroads into design during the previous decade.

It came as a direct result of a surge of enthusiasm for classical design.

19

5. *Tureen and ladle in the rococo style by George Wickes, c.1745.*

Exploration of the ancient sites of Herculaneum and Pompeii by English travellers, dilettanti and artists, who returned with sculpture and pottery, very soon became the subject of illustrated works. Interest was aroused beyond expectation. In England, the most influential figure was Robert Adam (1728–92), the architect and designer. He travelled in Italy during the 1750's, and when he returned to England was appointed architect to George III. The neo-classical period has become synonymous in England with the Adam period, for Robert Adam used all the classical ideas he had seen during his travels in the buildings he created. These were reflected in the interior decoration, in the furniture of the period and in the silver. Everything was complementary and in exquisite harmony.

It is not difficult to see why neo-classical design so quickly established itself, reigning supreme as it did from approximately 1770 until the end of the century, for everything about it was a delight to the eye, from its perfect regularity and symmetry to its light, graceful ornament. Silver lent itself particularly well to the neo-classical. The shape of vessels with their sweeping, flowing curves were sublimely elegant, perhaps vase shaped, tapering to the base on a slender stem, often delicately engraved with a pattern taken from the recently published illustrated works on the subject and including the Greek key pattern, bay leaf garland, acanthus leaves, running floral scrolls, rams' heads, ribbon bows and swags of foliage and cloth. Seldom, if ever, was such decoration over-applied, unlike rococo ornament which was sometimes rather encrusted.

Neo-classicism was in fashion at an important time for silver. It coincided with various advances in techniques which meant that silver could be rolled to a thinner gauge and produced for less cost. An enormous quantity of silver therefore poured from silversmiths made in the neo-classical fashion, far outnumbering the number of pieces made in the heavier more expensive silver of the rococo period. When the nineteenth century arrived the market had been flooded and it was ripe for a change.

The Regency period which followed saw the introduction of a variety of styles, many of which were heavy, very ornate and sometimes over-stated. Designers enjoyed themselves, but were often undisciplined, drawing eclectically on ideas from all over the world, including ancient Egypt, the Far and Near East, Greece and Imperial Rome. They also admired Gothic architecture which influenced various aspect of their design. Much domestic silver produced during the first two decades of the nineteenth century were still decorated by the Greek key design or foliate bands, but, alas, the shapes they adorned were usually no longer the graceful ones of the preceeding century.

Rococo decoration was reintroduced with C-scrolls, *rocaille* and floral ornament, but it generally lacked the brilliance and vitality of the original, although there were exceptions. Nonetheless, it became popular to such an extent that earlier, unembellished articles, including teapots and jugs, were returned by eager owners to the silversmith for embossing in the current rococo fashion.

Design and decoration were in an undecided state, therefore, by the time Queen Victoria ascended the throne. At this point naturalism emerged and with it an enthusiasm for excesses in decoration. Shapes and outlines were borrowed from preceding periods, but growingly lacked their fine proportions or better attributes, evolving into strange, exaggerated derivatives. Designers and craftsmen became besotted with naturalism, paying fanatical attention to detail of plants and flowers. By the 1840's, naturalism was all-embracing. It gathered momentum into the next decade, incorporating exotic tropical plants (the vine and modest periwinkle were becoming boring) and adding a newcomer, the palm tree, which lent a touch of tropical romance, perhaps shaped as supports for dishes or framing the periphery of an Arabic scene. These scenes and ideas evolved into a Moorish style. Although they delighted a certain sophisticated following, others remained faithful to less ornate naturalism, preferring a bunch of grapes around a border, succulent and convincing; leaves, acorns, giant lily and iris plants or oak trees and leaves.

The Victorians were also enamoured with Elizabethan and Gothic ideas. The former included heavy strapwork and the latter integrated the shapes to be found in Church architecture. Louis-Quatorze and Louis Quinze styles concentrated on rococo scrolls and floral motifs, interspersed with French decoration and design. There was also a classical Greek revival towards the middle of the century.

By the 1870's a new fashion emerged. Displays of Japanese art in London precipitated this, and now engravings which were strongly influenced by Japanese culture appeared on domestic silver. By the following decade, they adorned Japanese-inspired shapes, sometimes with handles formed to resemble bamboo.

Art Nouveau made its appearance in England around the last decade of the century. It was derived from an unusual combination of Japanese and medieval ideas. It shone out as something singular, brilliant and original. The wonderfully flowing lines upon which it was based with their sinewy, meandering curves were at direct contrast to the welter of borrowed ideas which the Victorians reproduced and over-embellished. *Art Nouveau* provided the long-felt need of something to stimulate interest in a new conception of design, and many progressive designers were quick to seize upon it as their source of inspiration. They included Charles Robert Ashbee (1863–1942), who had been a follower of William Morris, and who founded the School and Guild of Handicraft. The Guild produced much silver of a high calibre, some of which bears Ashbee's initials as he was the chief designer. *Art Nouveau* declined by around 1910, and was in evidence no more after the First World War.

Charles Robert Ashbee was prominent among the artist-craftsmen of the time who wished to return to the sort of craftsmanship which had originally made the

6. *Facing Page: A neo-classical vase-shaped mustard pot with applied beaded rim and beaded pedestal base by John Lambe, London, 1786. (The Colman Collection)*

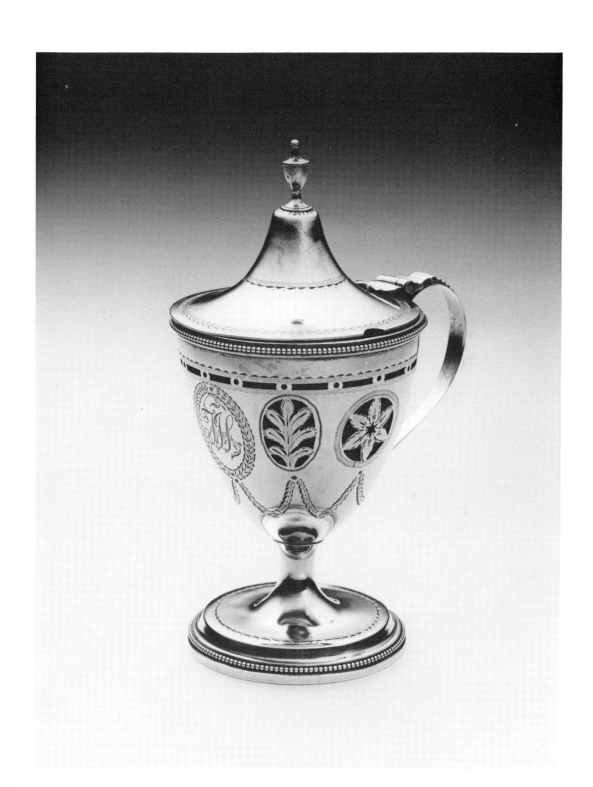

23

7.	*Nineteenth century naturalism is exemplified by this silver-gilt taperstick by Joseph Willmore, Birmingham, 1831. (Birmingham Assay Office)*

name of the London goldsmith one of such high repute. He turned away from the mass-production of the day and trained the Guild craftsmen to work in the old ways, hammering, raising, chasing and modelling. Thus silver produced by the Guild is unique for its period, being generally undecorated with its surface burnished to a soft sheen, showing hammer marks. Shapes were simple. Lines were pure, based on earlier forms. Ashbee also favoured the use of semi-precious stones and enamels.

However, creative designers like Ashbee had only a small influence on the manufacturers of silverware for the retail trade, even though Liberty and Company (founded 1875) encouraged artist-designers, including those who produced *Art Nouveau* designs, and had their own Cymric silver with a Celtic or Art Nouveau influence (1900).

Techniques

The reason why design continued on a generally non-original basis was one of economics. Mass-production techniques kept down costs and increased sales. This was why hand-worked silver had originally declined, and why it was no longer feasible when Ashbee and other purists tried to restore it. On the other hand, not everything was bad about mass-production. For one thing, it eliminated the heavy, arduous work suffered originally by the working silversmith who, before he could even begin to shape a vessel, needed by the sweat of his brow, to hammer the ingot into a malleable 'sheet'. Only after this would come the stage of forming the vessel by cutting round shapes from the 'sheet', and then raising these into the hollow forms of vessels. This was achieved by hammering on the sinking block which was shaped to fit the outlines of various vessel, or on stakes of iron or steel. It was important that the hammer had no sharp edges since this would have harmed the silver, and, because the metal developed a springy quality as it was worked, it was necessary to anneal it continuously.

When the craftsman had achieved the required shape of the vessel (which he would adeptly measure with calipers and gauges) he would polish the object with a broad-faced planishing hammer. This also eliminated any irregularities in the surface of the metal. Afterwards, handles, feet, finials or other supplementary parts which had been cast in moulds were soldered to the vessel. Some shapes, including tankards, might be made in two horizontal sections and soldered together. A vertical seam would be the method used in others.

Decoration was produced variously. The most general was that of engraving. A scorper, which was a small chisel with blades of different shapes, or graver would be deftly applied to cut decorative lines and patterns out of the metal, removing the silver as it was worked. Flat chasing produced a comparable effect, but was less distinct because it did not remove any metal. The craftsman hammered punches along the surface to produce the desired effect. Patterns which have been flat chased may be observed faintly on the reverse side of the metal.

Punching and embossing employed the same method but were applied on opposite sides of the silver. Punching – with a plain or shaped head – was worked on the side which is seen, while embossing necessitated the punches to be worked from the reverse side. More elaborate patterns, worked on the reverse of the metal, perhaps incorporating chasing, are termed *repoussé*.

Piercing, which seldom fails to look attractive, is the name used to describe the technique that involved the cutting away of small pieces of metal, leaving the remainder as a pattern. At one time this was achieved by the application of a fret-saw which was very time-consuming because the saw had to be sharpened so often since the steel was not sufficiently hard to stand the friction. Later, a harder steel was produced. This early form of piercing needed to be strengthened because a surplus of silver was removed and this was generally achieved by convex embossing.

However, by the 1770's, coinciding with the neo-classical fashion, big strides had been made in the techniques employed by the silversmith and the improvements in mechanisation resulted in a more efficient stamping machine which, by altering the punches, could be used to cut uncomplicated open-work patterns. This mechanised piercing was used for all sorts of objects including sugar baskets and fruit or cake baskets. The neo-classical motifs were soldered on by hand. Later, these, too, were integrated in the mechanised cut-out design. The steel tool which automatically pierced the sheet of silver was eventually made of a harder steel, as already mentioned, thus enabling longer runs and also making it possible to produce more interesting patterns.

Applied ornament, as its name implies, involved the soldering to the vessel or object of decoration cut from sheets of silver, or of decorative castings. Cut-card work which was much favoured by Huguenot silversmiths is an example of applied work. This was in fashion from around the last few years of the seventeenth century until approximately 1720 and, in its simplest form, consisted of foliate shapes.

The primitive method of hammering an ingot by brute force into a sheet of metal of the required gauge was superseded by the invention of the rolling-mill. The basic form of this English invention first made its appearance during the late seventeenth century and, although initially it did not much affect the manufacture of silver, all this was to alter in the eighteenth century. Compressing springs were placed on the upper of the two revolving cylinders so that an unheated ingot of silver could be passed through rollers and be flattened into a sheet of a consistent gauge. This meant that for the first time wares and miscellaneous objects could be produced in a far thinner silver, greatly lessening their cost since the weight of the silver and the time needed to produce the sheet from the ingot were reduced. The rolling-mill had far-reaching effects on the manufacture of silver wares. Its growing efficiency resulted in the production of progressively thinner silver and further reduction in costs.

Mass-production had arrived, for by now machinery could be used for stamping, piercing and embossing, and the thin silver produced by the rolling-mill was perfect for this automatic stamping by drop-hammers and fly-punches. Harder steel increased the rate at which domestic wares could be manufactured. A further innovation was the steam-powered rolling mill. Matthew Boulton and his partner John Fothergill pioneered this and from the 1770's used it with great effect. They produced vast numbers of unfinished, shaped parts. These were then purchased by silversmiths who would assemble them into the finished object. Pierced table baskets in particular lent themselves well to this method of manufacture, sometimes consisting of up to thirty segments, all of which had been previously automatically pierced by mechanisation. The prolific output of mass-produced domestic silver which now enamated from Sheffield and Birmingham caused the ultimate demise of the monopoly held by London silversmiths since medieval times, although pieces of quality, hand-made and finished were still produced by the London craftsmen.

One of the prettiest forms of decoration was introduced in the later years of the eighteenth century. It enhanced a wide miscellanea of objects, large and small, and was perfect for neo-classical ornament. It was called bright-cutting and is

8. *A Victorian child's christening set in the Japanese style. The egg cup and spoon by Elkington, 1880; the mug and bowl by E. C. Brown, 1880. (Phillips)*

easy to identify because of its interesting faceted effect. Basically it was engraving, the tool being inserted into the silver at varying angles. Tools of different sizes were used, sharpened similarly to a chisel, bevelled from corner to adjacent corner, with two cutting points. In this way all the charm of neo-classical decoration was emphasised and outlined by the sparkling, delicate incisions, perhaps a ribbon bow, swag of foliage or running floral scrolls.

The nineteenth century saw the advance of engine-turned ornament, which is not difficult to identify because of its over-all precision. The object to be decorated was turned on a lathe to give interesting textured effects. An assortment of patterns for small personal boxes in particular, like card cases and snuff boxes, was achieved by this method, many of which might also be adorned with other decorative effects, perhaps chased in high relief and engraved.

A much favoured form of ornament for card cases and vinaigrettes, among others, was the place of popular or historical interest. These are known as castle

9. *A mustard pot influenced by art nouveau in the style of pieces produced for Liberty's at that time. Birmingham, 1902. (The Colman Collection)*

tops among dealers. They have become avidly collected and are now costly. Their subjects are numerous and range from Crystal Palace to Windsor Castle.

Cutlery – generally called flatware – came slowly into use in England. For a long time the English ignored the fact that forks were used with benefit on the Continent, and remained loyal to their own primitive method which employed a spoon, knife and fingers. It was not until after the Restoration in 1660 that forks appear to have become more highly regarded and, little by little, more generally accepted. Queen Elizabeth I possessed in 1574 twelve spoons and "XII forks of silver and gilt, three of them broken". One of the earliest known silver table forks can be seen at the Victoria and Albert Museum, London. It is dated 1632, has a stem like a spoon and two prongs. Three prongs appeared during the 1680's and four prongs, as a general rule, by 1760–70's, although some four-pronged forks were also available far earlier.

Matching knives and forks with silver hafts were produced from the early years of the reign of George I, but with the advent of the efficient rolling-mill and its end product of thin silver, knives and forks were made by a cheaper method. From around the 1770's, the hafts were stamped out in vast numbers, die-struck in two parts and soldered together. Shellac was poured into the haft and the tang of the blade or fork inserted securely before this hardened. Business among Sheffield cutlers grew enormously as a result. Not until the early nineteenth century was the heavier gauge sometimes reintroduced, and most of these examples have plain, reeded hafts.

Box collecting – whatever the type of box – has a fascination of its own. The hinges of boxes warrant particular mention as these can be an indication of period. Until the early years of the eighteenth century hinges were generally of the knuckle-and-lug variety. The base of the box housed the former and the lid the latter. Base and lid were united by a traverse bolt. Thus the hinge stood away from the box. The eighteenth century hinge was moved away from the rim of the box towards the centre. By the nineteenth century the beautiful, integral hinge was in fashion. This type of hinge is a continuous joy to the collector of boxes because of the high degree of craftsmanship and expertise which has produced them. The hinge is often so meticulously concealed or disguised by decoration that it is difficult to detect. Such hinges were produced contemporaniously with boxes which possessed the usual hinge.

Sometimes hinges have been damaged. Before purchasing it is wise to examine in detail, by a good light, the working of the hinge. Open the box several times, ensuring that it closes smoothly. Any defects should reveal themselves and if too extreme the object should be disregarded.

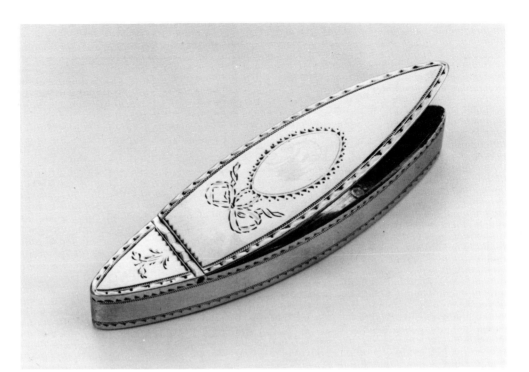

10. *A toothpick box by Samuel Pemberton, Birmingham, 1784, typically bright-cut with neo-classical motifs with the hinge concealed by decoration on the top of the box. (Birmingham Assay Office)*

CHAPTER 3

Boxes and Small Objects

Since boxes of all shapes and sizes, and for numerous purposes, have been used for hundreds of years, collecting boxes can provide a long, varied and stimulating pastime. Also, as with other items, a collection of less expensive boxes can be accumulated, then traded in for cash or swapped in part exchange when more expensive varieties are aspired to, which often happens to the collector who becomes immersed in the subject. Dealers are generally helpful and kindly disposed to trading-in, so, with this in mind, always try to purchase the best that you can afford. Badly damaged or dubious objects are best left on the shelf.

Boxes made from the last years of the eighteenth century emanated in vast quantities from Birmingham. These will therefore be punched with the Birmingham assay mark, which is an anchor (see chapter on hallmarks), and in all probability will have been made by one of the more prolific Birmingham silversmiths who, with their descendants, produced boxes in the thousands. Among such makers are the following: Samuel Pemberton and family, Matthew Linwood (the name Matthew Linwood is shared by six members of the family), Nathaniel Mills, Thomas Willmore and Joseph Taylor. Boxes were also made by silversmiths in others parts of the country, including those in London.

Card Cases

Card cases appeared in growing numbers from approximately the second decade of the nineteenth century, although they were known of earlier. They held visiting cards. They are in general around 4 in × 3 in, deep enough to hold a number of cards. They have hinged, slip-over covers and are variously decorated, sometimes with ornate patterns over-all, perhaps with a cartouche for the owner's initials. Hallmarks are generally found on the exterior of the rim at the top of the rectangular case. Those examples decorated by important places or buildings of interest, of which a wide variety exist, like all other boxes with this type of adornment, have become much sought after and are costly. Bargains may still be found in plain or less decorated versions, some of which are engine-turned. Towards the last few years of the nineteenth century the ornament of card cases came under the influence of *art nouveau*. Other designs were also produced including those with wavy edges, decorated with scrolls and foliate/floral patterns.

Counter Boxes

These survive from approximately 1650, although earlier, rare examples are known. They take the form of a small, cylindrical box around 1½ in high × 1 in diameter, perhaps smaller. They are very attractive, some having pierced sides and lids, others with pierced lids or lids embossed with the sovereign's bust, or some other type of decoration. They contained gaming counters which were used instead of money.

The counters might be decorated similarly to the cover, perhaps finely stamped with portraits of Kings and Queens, or resembling current coins. An Elizabethan example in the Victoria and Albert Museum, London, contains thirty-nine Elizabethan sixpences. Counter boxes do not always contain their original counters, and seldom have their full contingent, which varied but was commonly as many as twenty, and more. A late eighteenth century type of counter box – not very common – has its cover engraved with the numbers up to ten and a movable pointer.

Etui

An etui was a small, portable case usually with a hinged cover which contained items of necessity for specific purposes. The word is of French origin, and eighteenth century silversmiths became amusingly confused over its spelling. A 'tweezer' is the name given to it on one illustrated silversmith's trade card. Ladies might attach them to a chatelaine, and these would contain perhaps a pencil, scissors, a tiny spoon, bodkin and tweezers. A mid-eighteenth century example contains, among other things, a telescope, adjusted by moving the cover up and down its sleeve, and with shutters at either end to conceal the lenses safely. A gentleman's etui might incorporate a measure, instruments and a pencil; that for a doctor or surgeon a set of knives for letting blood. The campaign etui carried by soldiers had cutlery, condiment containers and a corkscrew. Whatever the contents, all fitted with minute precision into the case.

Needle Cases

The needle case is an obscure little object which has a habit of turning up where one least expects to find it. When this occurs the cost is often pleasingly low. Look out for a narrow, flattish case, approximately 3–4 in long by about ½in wide, with a pull-off cover. The case may taper slightly. The larger versions were intended for bodkins. Decoration is generally by engraving or bright-cutting, and, like the other boxes, needle cases were made in quantities by the Birmingham silversmiths.

Nutmeg Graters

Today the nutmeg is considered a humble spice, but this was not so in the times of our ancestors. It was both expensive and popular, and considered so flavoursome

11. *Nineteenth century card cases and vinaigrettes of the 'castle top' variety. (Harvey & Gore)*

that it warranted its own portable container so that a person might dispense it freshly ground into punch, mulled ales, hot negus, or anything else for which it might be considered desirable. It was favoured by both men and women during the eighteenth century and well into the nineteenth.

Early nutmeg graters made during the latter years of the seventeenth century were delectable little boxes, perhaps heart shaped or 'teardrop' in form. In common with successive boxes of various shapes they held one nutmeg and generally had two hinged 'lids', one at the top of the box and the other at the

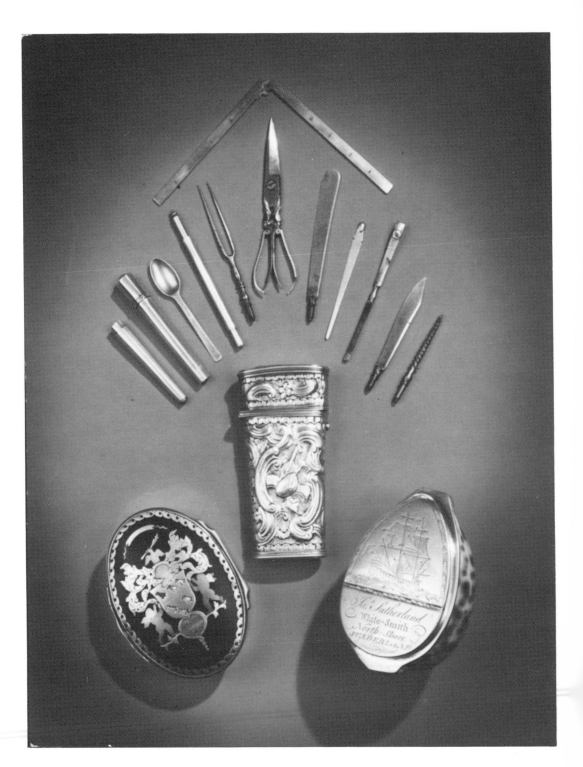

34

bottom, forming the base. A rasp was incorporated beneath the top lid and the nutmeg was housed below this, removed through the base of the box. A quick grating on the rasp would render a flow of the toothsome spice through the open base. A further design, tubular in form, had a separate cover and a removable rasp inside. Other types were also made. As with vinaigrettes, nutmeg graters were produced in a variety of forms and decorated variously. They were not always hallmarked during the eighteenth century and they were made as well in Sheffield plate from after the mid-eighteenth century.

Patch Boxes

Certain types of patches must have been a 'fun' form of cosmetic. I say 'fun', because surely nobody would have considered themselves made beautiful by the application of a patch in the shape of, perhaps, a fully masted ship sailing across the brow, or an opulent chateau perched between the eyebrows or on the cheek. The fashion for wearing patches first appeared in the French court, followed by the English court, and these larger examples were no doubt applied as the fashion became more extreme and the ladies competed with each other for the highlight.

One of the earliest hallmarked patch boxes is dated 1669, but the fashion for patches or 'court plasters', which was another name for them, is reckoned to be two or three decades earlier. Generally patches were not so exaggerated as those already mentioned. They were mostly regarded as beauty spots. They were usually made from small pieces of black velvet or silk shaped as spots, stars and crescents, stuck deftly on with mastic. ("Now vary'd patches wander o'er the face". John Gay, *The Fan,* 1714). The women of fashion in the eighteenth century were often experts in the art of cosmetics. Paint, patches and powder were generously applied and eyebrows were either plucked or supplemented with strips of mouse skin.

A small container was needed to house such adjuncts to beauty, therefore, and patch boxes became common during the eighteenth century. They were generally circular, from about 3/4 in diameter and approximately 1/2 in deep. Others might be larger. Their pull-off lids might be variously engraved, and the pattern, in such cases, would be repeated around the side of the box in moderation. The base, too, might be decorated. Patch boxes were also produced in other shapes, the more expensive versions perhaps being of silver-gilt. Hallmarks were punched inside the lid and on the base. Sheffield plate patch boxes were also made in quantity from its earliest period.

12. *Facing Page: Centre, an etui with contents, c.1740; left: 'pique-inlay' snuff box, eighteenth century; right: silver-mounted cowry-shell snuff box, eighteenth century. (Spink and Son Ltd.)*

Snuff Boxes

Snuff boxes were produced in an enormous number to cope with the habit of snuff taking which grew to reach epidemic proportions. This started at the beginning of the eighteenth century, although snuff had been introduced to Europe originally by the Spaniards, and grew increasingly during successive years. Snuff taking still lingers on today. The portable snuff box need never be confused with an early tobacco box, since it has one important difference – a hinged lid. This was necessary so that the taker of snuff might have a hand free for the vital pinch of this fashionable nasal stimulant. Larger snuff boxes, intended to be placed on a side table, did not usually have a hinged lid.

Snuff boxes were variously decorated, and followed all the changes in style and techniques prevalent throughout the eighteenth century and later. They were also made in Sheffield plate, popularly of a rectangular design, but often show signs of wear at the edges and corners, revealing the copper beneath. Both silver and Sheffield plate versions were naturally prone to much wear and tear, and therefore show corresponding signs of wear including dents and scratches or rubbed patterns. All had one thing in common, a really tightly fitting lid which was essential because snuff is sensitive to heat and moisture.

Stamp Boxes

These tiny, slender boxes were made from the nineteenth century and onwards. They contained postage stamps. Although they are still comparatively inexpensive, they may be overlooked because they are often jumbled together with a miscellany of objects and pass unnoticed. They are flat, 'envelope' like containers, roughly the size of a postage stamp, and sometimes have a ring attached so that they might be worn on the person. They are not without charm but probably would not warrant building an entire collection around, although they might be included in a collection of contemporaneous items in silver.

Tobacco Boxes

Tobacco was introduced into England towards the end of the sixteenth century and it is thought that in all probability earthenware containers were used to hold it. From approximately the time of the Restoration (1660), oval, silver boxes appeared and were in use increasingly during the years that followed. They were decorated in the style of the day and some were engraved with candles, pipes, bottles and the paper roll in which tobacco was bought. A suitable text, perhaps "Ne quid nimis" (nothing in excess) might also be incorporated. The popularity of oval tobacco boxes decreased around the middle years of the eighteenth century, although later examples do exist, and an out-of-period copy by Hester Bateman, c.1780, has a bright-cut and engraved 'wriggle-motif' lid with the owner's monogram. It is 4 in × 2⅜ in.

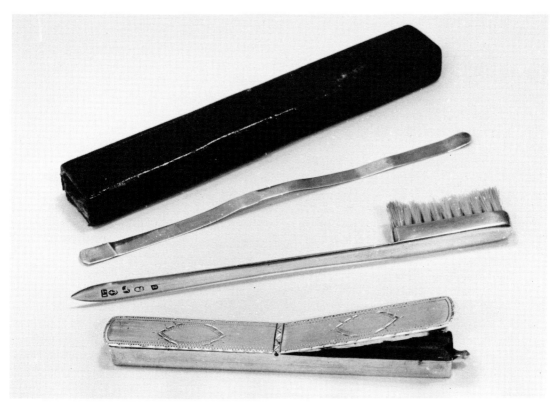

13. *Toothpowder box, toothbrush, tongue scraper and red morocco leather case.
Maker's mark, Joseph Taylor, Birmingham, 1797. (Birmingham Assay Office)*

Toothbrush Cases

Silver-handled toothbrushes developed during the later years of the eighteenth century, although they were made in a basic form far earlier. They generally incorporated a rectangular frame into which the brush could be fitted and removed for renewal or cleaning. In just the same way as we have plastic boxes for carrying toothbrushes today, the silver box or case came into being for the wealthy, perhaps plain or engraved, sometimes with the owners monogram, they were adorned by a variety of neo-classical motifs. A very rare type of toothbrush had a small container at the opposite end to the brush to hold toothpowder, which would have been better ignored since a seventeenth century recipe for toothpowder included pumice-stone, the shell of cuttle-fish, mother of pearl, coral and brown sugar. Perhaps this might account for the small demand for toothbrushes.

Toothpick Boxes

Toothpick boxes are generally attractive. Their size varies, but is commonly up to approximately $3\frac{1}{2}$ in $\times$ $\frac{1}{2}$ in deep. They are narrow, sometimes only about $\frac{1}{2}$ in wide, although others may be a pretty elliptical shape, and in which case they are often bright-cut and engraved with more elaborate patterns than the very simple variety. Others may have cut corners. Beautifully concealed hinges in the pattern on the lid often adds greatly to their merit.

Vesta Boxes

The vesta box was a nineteenth century innovation, introduced out of necessity around the middle of the century. Vesta matches appeared during the third decade or so of the nineteenth century and were extremely combustible. Because of this it was essential to carry them in some sort of container for safety. Not long elapsed before an appropriate case was devised, but until that time they might be carried in a snuff box incorporating a rasp, on which the match was struck. Vesta boxes are approximately 2 in long $\times$ $1\frac{1}{2}$ in, perhaps $\frac{1}{2}$ in deep, although their sizes vary. They have slip-on hinged covers. They are generally hallmarked on the rim at the top. Many are quite plain. Others are variously decorated and there are as well those formed as a novelty shape, perhaps pigs, fish, books, Brazil nuts or musical instruments. A certain type also has a compartment for sovereigns. They generally incorporated a ring so that they might be worn.

Vinaigrettes

The name vinaigrette originates from the aromatic vinegar of the eighteenth century used to divert the sense of smell from the more unpleasant odours of the day. The piquant, aromatic vinegar had strong acetic acid as its basis which was mixed with an assortment of ingredients including oils of lavender, cinnamon, fragrant quince, lemon, cloves and camphor. A quick whiff of this was sufficient to dispel any feelings of nausea since many of the more earthy smells stood little chance against it. To this day, the aroma my linger still on the original sponges sometimes found in vinaigrettes.

Vinaigrettes are small boxes, perhaps as tiny as approximately 1 in square by $\frac{1}{2}$ in deep. At first they were called by the prosaic name of aromatic vinegar boxes, which gave no chance for confusion. However, towards the end of the eighteenth century, the more fanciful name of vinaigrette came into being and remained until these charming little boxes went out of fashion, and were gradually replaced after around the mid-nineteenth century by various forms of the smelling bottle.

The lids of vinaigrettes are always hinged and earlier examples made in the late eighteenth century and early nineteenth are usually far smaller than succeeding designs. Upon opening the lid one discovers what looks like another inner lid, pierced, often in a delightful pattern and gilded. Earlier vinaigrettes usually have more simple piercing. Their lids are also less ornate. Beneath the hinged, pierced

14. *Nineteenth century vinaigrettes. (J. H. Bourdon-Smith Ltd.)*

inner 'lid' would be placed a small piece of sponge, thoroughly soaked in aromatic vinegar. Its perfume would waft through the pierced holes when the outer lid was open and its owner could partake for a few brief moments of the delights of this early form of air freshener.

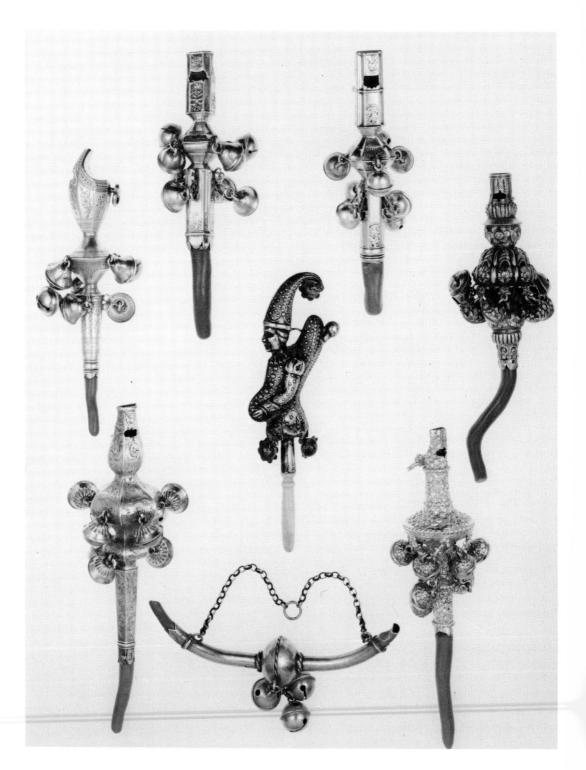

40

Engraving and bright-cutting were the main form of decoration on earlier vinaigrettes, lending a delicate air to these tiny boxes. Vinaigrettes grew in size during the nineteenth century and became rather substantial. New shapes and designs appeared and, as well as including the more usual oval, round and rectangular forms (sometimes with shaped edges), embraced an amazing diversity of novelty ideas among which were books, purses with or without handles, hearts, bellows, thistles, bottles, strawberries, cannons, crowns (made to celebrate the Coronation of George IV), snails, policeman's lamps, beehives and flowers. A fish was actually joined and articulated – now very rare – with the aromatic sponge contained in its head.

After about 1830 vinaigrettes often incorporated a small ring, so that they might be worn on a chain, and also from approximately this time 'castle top' vinaigrettes became popular (many by Nathaniel Mills) depicting buildings of historical interest like St. Paul's Cathedral, Newstead Abbey, Warwick Castle and the Dublin Exhibition Building of 1853. Vinaigrettes are almost always hallmarked. These may appear inside the inner lid, on the inside of the base and sometimes a lion passant on the pierced inner 'lid'. Marks generally include the maker's initials.

Baby Rattles

Silver, silver-gilt and sometimes gold mounted rattles, commonly with a piece of coral at one end, and a number of small bells and sometimes a whistle, have been made for generations. In 1690 the 1st Earl of Bristol records that he paid £1.10s for a 'corrail set in gold'. The Prince Regent used an exquisite gold rattle decorated in the rococo style and made in 1760, which still has its original shagreen case. Queen Victoria possessed another beautiful example also with a coral teether and six bells, which was made in 1806 and subsequently passed on to her children and grandchildren.

The royal family were not the only ones to have these delightful objects. Similar rattles in silver were made in large numbers in the eighteenth and nineteenth centuries. They usually incorporated a length of coral because this was said to sooth the inflamed gums of teething infants, and also was supposed to possess a mystic quality which acted as an antidote to evil. Later, ivory or mother-of-pearl might replace the coral. Rattles were generally beautifully decorated in the style of the day. Those made during the final years of the eighteenth century might be adorned with neo-classical motifs, bright-cut or engraved. Hand-decorated rattles declined during the late Victorian era and mass-produced, stamped out counterparts began to take their place. Later came moulded animals, bunnies or

15. Facing Page: Baby rattles in a variety of styles, incorporating bells, whistles and teething coral. (Phillips)

ducklings and nursery rhyme characters. Silver rattles should be hallmarked. Often every small part is marked, the mount, the whistle, the bells and the tiny ring through which a ribbon would have been threaded so that the rattle could be tied within the infant's reach. Each might bear a lion passant.

Bookmarkers

Bookmarkers have been copied extensively in modern times. They are usually blade shaped in outline with a decorative, sometimes novelty handle. Around the periphery of the 'blade', a tiny distance from the edge, the silver is cut away so that the 'blade' may be slipped through a page, leaving the handle to protrude as the marker. Made mostly during the later years of the nineteenth century and into the twentieth century, they are interesting to collect because of the diversity of their handles.

Buckles

Buckles were a vital part of the dress from the late seventeenth century and increasingly throughout the entire eighteenth century. They adorned not only the wealthy (both men and women) but also those of less affluent means, although not necessarily in silver. Their size and shape varied according to what was in fashion at the time, and the size was sometimes so extreme as to render the simple buckle ludicrous. Buckles were made for shoes, belts, breeches (at the knee), hats and socks. They were produced in silver, gold, white metal and pinchbeck, commonly set with paste jewels or diamonds for the wealthy. They were seldom fully hallmarked until the end of the eighteenth century, unless they were very large. It is usual for only the rim to be of silver and the tongue to be made of steel. Buckles can be very attractive and may still be purchased quite reasonably. Having acquired them, though, they must become part of a collection, for they are seldom easy to wear with the garments of this century.

Buttons

From the last two decades or so of the sixteenth century the very wealthy used buttons of jewelled gold and these were latterly joined by buttons of less precious metal. After a while more than forty master button-makers were working in the City of London, producing buttons of silver, pewter, tin and brass. Until about 1720 hallmarks were struck on the face of buttons, but following this it is comparatively rare to find hallmarks until after 1790 when they were generally struck on the reverse. After this date hallmarks became more usual because buttons were no longer exempt from assaying.

Sketchley's Birmingham Directory, 1767, described the local button-making trade as very productive (silver, plated, gilt, lacquered and pinchbeck), and by 1770 more than 80 master button-makers were noted. They were joined later by a dozen or so specialists in Sheffield plate stamped buttons. This was as a result of

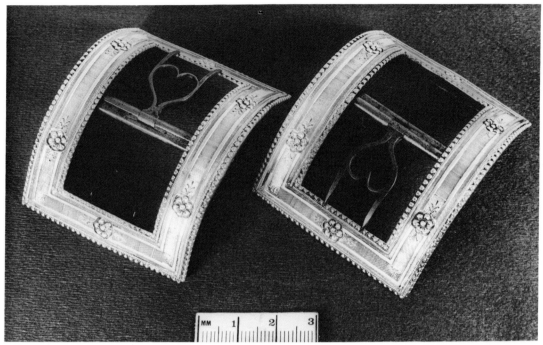

16. *Pair of shoe buckles by Thomas Willmore, Birmingham, 1799. (Birmingham Assay Office)*

the expiry of Richard Ford's patent for shaping buttons by a die stamp which stopped the metal from splitting.

Buttons made of silver, gold and Sheffield plate may be found in sets of six, eight or more. They were produced in countless patterns. Hunting buttons might have a fox mask in relief with the name of the hunt engraved around the edges; there are sets of racing buttons often dating from the Regency period; shooting and cockfighting buttons; and livery buttons, decorated with crests in high relief or engraved with a coat-of-arms or a crest. Other buttons were sold plain to local engravers who would add designs and inscriptions to commission.

Button Hooks

The button hook was all-apparent from approximately the mid-nineteenth century until the first two or three decades of the twentieth century. It was vital for fastening buttons on gloves, footwear and other articles of apparel which were often stitched to fabric in such a way as to render them almost impossible to manipulate with the fingers. Button hooks were made in varying sizes to accommodate the diameter of the button, and some have more than one hook for the same reason. Silver-handled button hooks – shafts were of steel – have become increasingly collectable, yet prices are still reasonable. They are generally

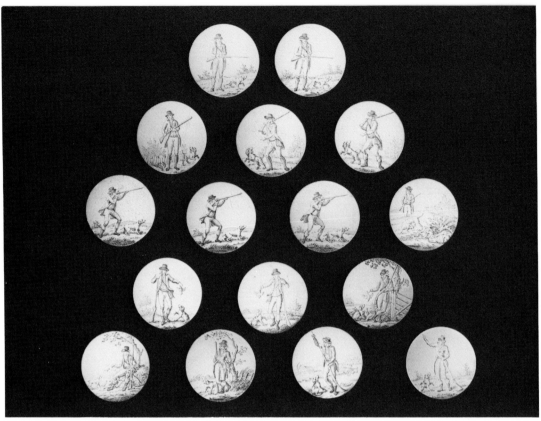

17. Set of sixteen buttons engraved with sportsman scenes by Thomas Willmore, Birmingham, 1790. (Birmingham Assay Office)

embossed in over-all patterns of rococo swirls and floral and foliate designs. They should be hallmarked, but these are sometimes a little difficult to find amidst the plethora of embossing.

Châtelaines

This useful object was once a commonplace necessity for holding an assortment of items. It was a simple device, consisting of a clip (for belt or girdle) from which hung small chains, to which were affixed the required items. For the lady of the house these might include a needle case, thimble in its 'bucket', memo pad, scissors in a safety sheath, keys, stamp or pill box. Clips might be decorated or plain. An early eighteenth century châtelaine might be of gold, exquisitely

18. Facing Page: châtelaine by George Unite, Birmingham, 1901. (Mallory of Bath)

45

embossed and chased with matching attachments. Later, silver châtelaines became quite general, their accoutrements nicely worked and often charming. They were usually hallmarked.

Pin Cushions

Pin cushions were sometimes found in toilet sets, although during the nineteenth century the ingenuity of their designs probably meant that these pretty and useful objects were sold individually and in some quantity. Apart from oval or round cushions, they were produced in a variety of novelty shapes including a lady's slipper, hearts, piglets, cows, chicks, owls, elephants and caskets. The cushion was set inside the silver shape, often of a diminutive size which added to their appeal. Until about a hundred years ago the steel from which pins were produced easily rusted when exposed to the air, and because of this the cushion of earlier examples might be stuffed with an abrasive, probably emery powder, so that the pins and needles were cleaned during their insertion. Beware the modern copy.

Thimbles

Examples of thimbles are extant from the sixteenth century. The Victoria and Albert Museum, London, has a silver-gilt specimen c.1710 with a suspension ring attached for use with a châtelaine. Many were made in other metals and alloys during the eighteenth century and those in silver may not be hallmarked, since the Plate Offences Act of 1738 included thimbles among the smaller articles exempt from assay. Thimbles became thinner towards the end of the eighteenth century and because of this may have tiny holes caused by wear from pins and needles. Hold the thimble up to a good light to detect these punctures. Thimbles were variously decorated and nineteenth century examples might incorporate moralising, advertising or commemorative inscriptions. Henry Griffith and Company of Birmingham made a prolific number of silver thimbles in a wide assortment of decorative patterns from 1856 until 1956. *Thimble buckets* (see Châtelaines) were attractive bucket-shaped containers, sometimes pierced, to hold the thimble when it hung from its chain on a châtelaine. They generally had two small rings for the silver chain.

CHAPTER 4

Spoons, Flatware, General Utensils

The spoon ranks as one of the most ideal of all items of silver to collect. Spoons are not only plentiful but also diverse, interesting and comparatively inexpensive in certain forms. Many have the additional advantage that they may be used. Collectors of spoons may take their choice from special purpose spoons; spoons with a particular type of decoration; spoons made by a specific silversmith; spoons made during a certain period; spoons for the table; or ancient spoons, once used by a proud owner centuries ago and now cherished as precious collectors' items.

Into the latter category must go early spoons with distinctive and decorative knop finials gracing the terminal of their stems. Such finials gave a certain primitive charm to spoons until approximately some years after the Restoration (1660). There were several forms, apart from those which might have been derived from family crests or in some way associated with the owners. For example, in the sixteenth century the Vintners' Company had a bunch of grapes as the appropriate knop of some of their spoons. Likewise from 1657, the Innholders' Company required the gift of a spoon on admission, and these bore the figure of St. Julian the Hospitaller.

One of the earliest spoon knops was the diamond point, in effect a simple pyramid shape. Certain examples have hallmarks punched during the reign of Henry VIII. The acorn knop was mentioned in fourteenth century wills, but was seldom made after about the fifteenth century. The writhen knop (approximately 1480–1550), consisted of a spherical shape marked with spiral twistings, while the woodwose was a wildman with a club, either swinging it or holding it against his shoulder. The woodwose appeared on spoons between roughly 1450 and 1600 and is mentioned in a sixteenth century will quite distinctly: "one dozen sylver spoons of the wylld man, gylte on the ends", valued at £4.3.4. An example dated about 1460 may be seen in the Victoria and Albert Museum.

Other knop finials included a moor's head, an owl, a boar's head, a seal top (a flat disc) and the maidenhead. One of the earliest maidenhead spoons probably dates from the fourteenth century (Victoria and Albert Museum) and is marked in the bowl with a coat of arms, thought to be that of the See of Coventry. Christ's Hospital, Horsham, has a set of twelve of 1630, which is near the final years of the maidenhead knop, for it ceased around the mid-seventeenth century.

Apostle spoons – with the apostle formed as the knop – were made in sets of thirteen, the thirteenth spoon being that of the figure of Christ in Majesty. They were also made singly, since it was the custom to give an apostle spoon as a

Christening present. One of the earliest sets dates from 1527, and the earliest part-set are the six Beaufort Spoons of c.1460. Apostle spoons have been copied copiously over the years.

Gradually the spoon began to change its shape. By the seventeenth century the slipped-in-the-stalk spoon had appeared. The stem of this was terminated by a cut at an oblique angle, upon which might be pricked the owner's initials. This evolved into the stump-end spoon and thence into the Puritan spoon, the latter being an important stage in the development of the spoon, since after this, instead of a decorative knop, the stem-end ornament usually consisted only of decoration on the flat end of the actual stem.

By the time Charles II had been restored to the throne the trifid-end spoon had appeared. The end of the stem was flattened and two short notches were cut, downwards towards the bowl, dividing the end of the stem into three sections, two small ones with a large central lobe. The stem and bowl junction was strengthened with a short V-shaped tongue. Other trifid spoons, usually later, might have the notches at the end of the stem cut so that the three parts were equal. The stem and bowl became strengthened at the back of the bowl by a tapering rib which was the early form of the rat-tail, fashionable for many years.

Towards the end of the seventeenth century, the back of the bowl was often decorated with foliated scroll work, hammered in low relief. The rat-tail was the central part of the design. Perhaps the front of the stem might be decorated in a complementary fashion. Others were unadorned, or might have the family crest or the owner's initials. In general the length of these spoons ranged from 6½ in for the smaller size to 7½ – 8½ in for the larger. By the last years of the century the trifid shape became less pronounced and the cuts forming the trifid disappeared, resulting in what is known as the wavy-end spoon. This had a distinct central curve with a small one either side. It was destined to remain only a short while before the decorative stem end finally evolved, as with the general shape of the spoon, into the utensil which we know today.

Within a decade or two after the turn of the eighteenth century, the stem of the spoon became curved and ended in a slightly rounded form which turned in the same direction as the concave of the bowl. This was known as the Hanoverian pattern which retained the rat-tail rib at the back of the bowl until about 1730. After about this time the rat-tail disappeared, to be replaced by a single or double drop. which, during the rococo period was often replaced in its turn by a shell, flower or scroll, cast or stamped in relief.

Another three decades were to pass before a further, and what is generally regarded as the final stage in the evolution of the shape of the stem, took place. The Old English pattern was introduced in 1760 which meant that the end of the stem was now turned downwards, that is, it ended in a curve in the opposite

19. *Facing Page: Left: seventeenth century diamond knop spoon; right: fifteenth century acorn knop spoon. (Phillips)*

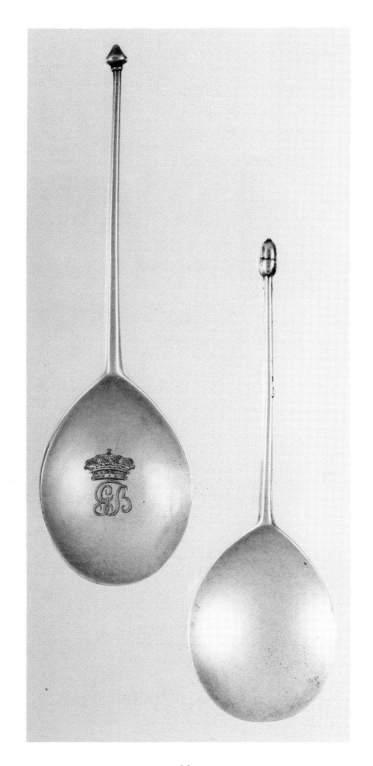

direction to that of the bowl of the spoon. It became the standard shape and has been followed in general ever since.

In general it can be said that spoons made prior to approximately the mid-eighteenth century are costly, particularly those with decorative knops, apostle spoons and trifid or wavy-ends, which are all collectors' items. However, the eighteenth century then gradually saw the introduction of all the specific purpose spoons with which we are all today well acquainted. These became increasingly more numerous because of advances in mass-production techniques, and therefore may still be collected today at realistic prices. New decorative patterns on the stems were introduced which means that the collector may choose from these and build up an entire collection in the same pattern.

The Onslow pattern, which was named after Arthur Onslow, (1691–1768), Speaker of the House of Commons for thirty-three years was introduced before the mid-eighteenth century, and must have caused considerable impact when it first appeared. It is extremely distinguished, ending at the end of the stem in a curled and reeded volute, the line of which is integrated into the stem. Sometimes it might be combined with a delicate feather edging. The latter was used a great deal and although simple was very effective, comprising an engraved border or outline of short, slight and oblique cuts. Threaded edges and beaded edges were similarly popular, the former appearing commonly on plain tapering stems as well as the fiddle pattern, a late eighteenth century introduction. This consisted of square shoulders either side of the bowl of the spoon, balanced by a complementing pair of square shoulders towards the end of the stem. It might be plain or decorated variously with thread and shell (a plain, narrow border terminating in a shell motif at the end of the stem) or the king's or queen's pattern.

Tea Spoons

Early, rare examples date from the last quarter of the seventeenth century. They have trifid finials, are small and might be gilded. They usually bear only the maker's mark. Tea spoons came only very gradually into general circulation, and up until the first four decades of the eighteenth century sets of tea spoons were still rare.

One distinct type of tea spoon, produced during the eighteenth century is known as the picture-back spoon. The back of the bowl of such spoons is decorated by a pattern or a picture, of which there are many versions, all rather similar, yet produced by a variety of silversmiths. This has given root to the supposition that the picture might have originated in some sort of pattern book for spoon makers to copy, but there does not seem to be any documentation to support this theory. Picture-back spoons became more prolific after about 1760. Their die-struck or cast embellishment might incorporate a farmyard scene; a

20. *Facing Page: Eighteenth century picture-back spoons. (Victoria and Albert Museum)*

teapot; a wheatsheaf (surmounting the word 'plenty'); a fully rigged galleon; an 'I love liberty' motif (the words surmounting an open birdcage upon the top of which is a bird with outstretched wings); a stork holding a serpent; and a dove with an olive branch in its beak. These are only a selection of the diverse subjects.

Snuff Spoons

These tiny, almost toy-like spoons were generally miniatures of the contemporary table spoon. They are charming. From about 1740 they were sometimes supplied as part of a lady's etui. Occasionally a snuff box is found with a clip on its lid or a special section intended to house one of these tiny spoons.

Mustard Spoons

Mustard spoons appeared in general during approximately the third quarter of the eighteenth century. The bowl was elongated, rather like a fig. Originally mustard spoons were intended to be used with dry mustard, since wet mustard pots made earlier than about 1765 were uncommon. The stems of mustard spoons followed the styles and patterns of contemporary spoons, but in general they tended to be rather plain.

Salt Spoons

Salt spoons were not necessary at one time since salt was taken on the blade of the knife. The early eighteenth century saw an enlightened approach to table manners, however, and with it came the use of the salt spoon. The bowls at first were commonly formed like small shovels, although some were circular. An unmarked example with a shallow, circular bowl and a ribbon-scrolled stem in the possession of the Exeter Museum is thought to have been made during the first ten years of the eighteenth century. As the years passed salt spoons became far more numerous until they finally became the accepted thing. They echoed the patterns of contemporary spoons. Early finials were Hanoverian and after about 1760 of the old English form. Salt spoons might have plain or gilded bowls: fluted with an Onslow terminal; engraved at the end of the stem with the owner's monogram or initials; and, into the nineteenth century, often intricately ornate with shell-shaped bowls and elaborately cast stems. Salt spoons are still reasonable in price.

Dessert and Table Spoons

By the turn of the eighteenth century and during the first two decades, varying sizes of spoons for specific purposes at table became apparent. This distinction included the table and dessert spoon, which were identical in every way except size. Before c.1770 specific services were produced for the dessert, but they were rare, often of gilt and extremely costly. After this they became more general and less expensive. Those who love old silver on the table might buy one or two Georgian table spoons (it does not matter if they do not match), since they look so handsome when the table is laid formally.

Berry Spoons

Beware the berry spoon! These are not of very ancient origin even though some may tend to look it. The berry spoon was introduced generally during the nineteenth century and became popular as a pretty spoon to be used with fruit. They are heavily ornate, embossed with suitable naturalistic decoration and have gilded bowls. Their popularity continued into the twentieth century. They are difficult to buy because spoons of earlier vintage have been converted into either single or pairs of berry spoons, and thus boast their original hallmarks. This can mislead the unwary.

Egg Spoons

The egg spoon is similar in shape of bowl to the mustard spoon, but was hardly used before the late eighteenth century. Egg spoons also came as part of an egg frame. Because egg discolours silver the bowls of egg spoons were gilded.

Medicine Spoons

Various forms of the medicine spoon are known. One of the earliest is like a dessert spoon with a short stem. It is thought that these appeared during the mid-eighteenth century. Another has a covered bowl with a hinged lid and tubular stem, commonly described as a castor-oil spoon which came into use around the first twenty years or so of the nineteenth century, although one later example of 1827 bears the signature of S. Gibson and adds 'inventor'. The tubular stem was hollow with an opening at the end. The dreaded castor oil was poured in, a finger then stopped up the opening and the oil was dispatched speedily into the mouth of the recipient through a hole in the covered bowl. A double-bowled medicine spoon also existed, a bowl being at either end of the stem, and each a different size. This type came into use from about the 1760's.

Basting Spoons

These large, heavy spoons which originated in the late seventeenth and eighteenth centuries were probably used for serving at table and basting in the kitchen. Some have turned wooden handles and others have pierced bowls. Many are merely the current style of spoon in circulation at the time, but very much larger. Large spoons were common in Scotland. Examples date from the early eighteenth century and seem to have been made in many of the towns where silver was produced. They were known as 'hash spoons'.

53

Sucket Spoons

These are hundreds of years old and appear in the inventory of King Edward VI, 1549. They take the form of a spoon with a two-pronged form at the opposite end of the stem. Sometimes the fork had three prongs. The purpose of this little implement was to spear up the sweet, sticky delights of the day, in the same way as a small disposable plastic fork is contained in a box of stem ginger or Turkish delight today. They are small, usually about five or five and a half inches in length.

Marrow Spoons

Closely related to the marrow scoop and generally thought to be its predecessor, the marrow spoon was simply a normal sized dessert spoon with the end of its stem shaped and grooved as a scoop. One of the earliest recorded is dated 1692. Up until the early years of the eighteenth century they usually have only a maker's mark, after which time they are generally fully marked.

Mote Spoons or Skimmers

The mote spoon is one of the small items of silver which were commonplace at the eighteenth century tea table. It looks like a tea spoon with a pierced bowl, with a slender, tubular stem, slightly tapering, which ends in a point. Its purpose was one which is now fulfilled by the tea strainer (this did not make its appearance until the final years of the eighteenth century and beginning of the nineteenth century). The mote skimmer was used to do the job before tea was poured from the pot into the cup, skimming off unwanted matter, while the point was applied to the perforations in the teapot spout since the leaves, which were then unbroken, commonly blocked these.

Early examples have simple pierced bowls; later specimens were more ornate, usually pierced with crosses and scrolls. The mote skimmer might be sold singly or in sets, or *en suite* with tea spoons. The *London Gazette* for 1697 describes "Long or strainer tea-spoons with narrow pointed handles". Later they were described variously as long tea spoons, strainer spoons and stirrer spoons. They were a little longer than a tea spoon which accounts for the first description. Early mote spoons have a rat-tail strengthening at the back of the perforated bowl, stretching from the stem. Later examples might have a single drop, double drop, shell or perhaps both, instead of the rat-tail.

Because of the slender, rather fine circular stem of the mote skimmer, it is often difficult to read the hallmarks. Very early examples quite commonly have only the maker's mark and the lion's head erased; a maker's mark and a lion passant is usual on later skimmers. Sometimes mote skimmers have been adapted from tea spoons and can be difficult to detect, but the slightly shorter length of stem usually reveals this.

Also made were large table-spoon size skimmers. They usually have George III

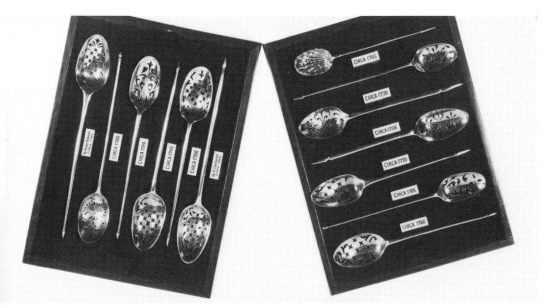

21. A collection of eighteenth century mote skimmers. (S. J. Shrubsole Ltd.)

hallmarks and it is thought that they were used when tea urns were in fashion. Others might have a marrow scoop instead of a point at the end of the stem and were about seven inches long. They were probably an adaptation of the mote skimmer.

Mote skimmers have increased in price over recent years but they are still numerous and make an interesting addition to a collection of spoons, or items relevant to the English habit of taking tea. Most dealers of repute should be able to show the collector one or two mote skimmers from stock.

Caddy Spoons

Early tea canisters usually had domed lids and these were used as a measure for the dry leaves, but as the tea canister gradually changed its shape a separate spoon or ladle became necessary. The first ladle generally had a deep, shell-shaped bowl from which the stem rose nearly vertically. Sometimes a small hook might be attached to the back of the stem, and this would be used to hang it in the tea chest. The stem might be of another material, perhaps ebony or black-stained boxwood. This type of ladle was probably in use from approximately 1745.

When tea canisters with wide lids became more general, a new form of ladle appeared which was kept in the canister with the tea. This was the short-stemmed variety which was introduced in about 1770, and which, by the end of the next decade or so, was being produced in increasing numbers, particularly by Birmingham silversmiths. Caddy spoons of this type continued to be made in vast quantities for the next seventy years or so, and, despite the fact that they performed a very small function, and that they were in themselves comparatively unimportant items in the homes of our predecessors, they grew increasingly in individuality and became popular as small presents. Because of this much thought and ingenuity went into their designs and they can truly be said to be a wonderful example of the silversmith's creativity and skill.

They were made simply, sometimes worked up from a sheet of silver (usually earlier examples), or the ladle bowl might be die-struck and the handle pressed, then the two pieces soldered together by hand. Others might be stamped in a single piece or, from about 1820, often cast. They were not exempt from hallmarking, despite their light weight. Caddy spoons made during the eighteenth century tended to be a little delicate and because of this often broke at the junction of the bowl and the stem. Many have, therefore, been repaired but such repairs are often hardly visible. Decoration and ingenious ornament abounded on caddy spoons. There are those of filigree or simulated filigree (seldom hallmarked because it is too fragile); others which were embossed, fluted, engraved or simple and plain; those which were gilded and others with their bowls shaped as shells.

There was an astonishing selection of other shapes. The jockey cap was foremost among these, and has become much sought after by collectors. It has been copied a great deal. Serious collectors often prefer the hallmarks to have been punched on the visor (which forms the handle) and naturally these should be of the appropriate period. Jockey caps varied. They might be plain or very simply engraved; have a ribbed cap and peak; be die-stamped and decorated with geometric patterns; or perhaps be engraved and bright-cut on the peak. The latter is charming and delicate, often with the cap segmented and a pretty embellishment of bright-cutting on the crown of the cap (possibly a star or snowdrop), which complements the bright-cut peak with its foliate or floral decoration. Joseph Taylor, Birmingham, among others, was well-known for his superlative jockey cap caddy spoons.

Caddy spoons produced during the later years of the eighteenth century and earlier years of the nineteenth century are among the more delicately embellished. As the nineteenth century progressed they became heavier and more ornate. Popular designs included a vine leaf with a bunch of grapes in the centre, the handle formed as a vine tendril in silver wire; a tea leaf with chased veins and a little stalk fashioned from a small twirl of wire; a circular 'frying-pan' bowl; a scoop shape; a shovel bowl; a stirrup design; and a bowl formed as a hand. There were those cast as crinoline ladies, Chinese mandarins, and fishermen with shells. Others originated as war trophies and incorporated a standard, pennon, cannon and ramming irons, drum and fife, bayonet and sword. They were made from approximately 1805–1815. Sometimes the stem might be engraved with the name of a victory.

Although caddy spoons were made in great numbers by Birmingham silversmiths including, apart from those already mentioned, Matthew Linwood, Samuel Pemberton, Cocks and Bettridge, and George Unite, many were also produced in Sheffield, London and Dublin. Irish caddy spoons were generally

22. *Caddy spoons, centre: William IV rococo die-stamped leaf, George Unite, Birmingham, 1834; left to right: George III shaped, elongated leaf with bright-cut handle, Thomas Wallis, London, 1800; George III grape-and-vine leaf by Matthew Linwood, Birmingham, 1819; George III pierced bowl, George Baskerville, London 1796; George III ribbed leaf, tendril handle, Wardell and Kempson, Birmingham, 1816; Victorian silver-gilt floral rococo leaf, cast finial, Hilliard and Thomasson, Birmingham, 1852.*

larger than either their English or Scottish counterparts. Makers in Sheffield included Daniel Holy, Richard Morton and Tudor and Leader; London was led by the Bateman family and included Edward Farrell, John Foligno and Phipps and Robinson; Dublin makers were James le Bass, Samuel Neville and John Osborne; and those from Edinburgh included William Cunningham, George Fenwick and John Ziegler. The assay offices of York, Exeter, Chester and Glasgow also struck a certain number of caddy spoons.

Some caddy spoons have handles of a different material which might be mother-of-pearl, stained wood or ivory. These have often been repaired at the

23. *Caddy spoon by Francis Clarke, Birmingham, 1828. (Birmingham Assay Office)*

24. *Francis Clarke's mark (one of four) was entered on July 12th, 1826. Left to right: the lion passant, the sovereign's head duty mark, the maker's initials, the anchor (mark of origin of the Birmingham Assay Office), the date letter 'C' for 1826. (Birmingham Assay Office)*

junction of the handle and bowl. Caddy spoons declined in popularity after about 1860 by when their ingenuity was less apparent, but they were still produced in a modified way and interesting shapes have been copied throughout successive years.

Ladles

Various types of ladles were in use during the eighteenth century and later, each of which was intended for a specific purpose. Such a vital utensil would have far earlier associations, of course, but the type, roughly which we recognise today, dates from around the second decade of the eighteenth century.

One of the earliest examples of the ladle has a pear-shaped bowl and curved, tubular handle with either a bird's or a beast's head at its terminal. These were generally supplied with a magnificent soup tureen made by prominent silversmiths of the day, among them Paul de Lamerie and George Wickes.

There were as well smaller ladles which might be sold en suite with sauce boats and sauce tureens. These, together with soup ladles, became far more common after about 1760, and then their stem terminals might be decorated by the Onslow pattern which looked handsome. From approximately 1770 small, light ladles appeared with pierced bowls (sifters) for use with sugar, while those without pierced bowls would have been made to use with cream pails or jugs.

A further type of ladle was used for punch or other alcoholic based drinks. Such a ladle would accompany the splendid punch bowl and early examples would be of heavy solid silver, including the long handles, the terminals of which would be decorative or matching those of contemporary spoons. Other eighteenth century examples were far less weighty, however, and many had handles of turned ivory, ebony, whalebone or wood.

Generally until approximately 1730 the bowl of the punch ladle was hemispherical, with or without an everted rim, and seldom lipped. Many were plain, but others might be embossed with floral and scroll designs and might incorporate a cartouche for an engraved crest. After approximately this date, bowls were shaped variously and included the goose-egg design (it is thought because the more pointed end of the ovoid was useful when pouring punch into goblets with a more narrow rim than had formerly been used), which might be plain or elaborately chased. Others had circular or oval bowls, beaten from discs of silver, the rims perhaps formed into a single pouring lip at right angles to the handle, again left absolutely plain or decorated. There were those which were lobed and fluted with double lips, while bowls shaped like nautilus shells appeared around the 1750's.

By this time also there was a fashion for forming the bowl from crown pieces so that the marginal design (or inscription) appeared around the bowl rim. Sometimes an earlier coin might be incorporated in the base of the bowl, which accounts for the mystifying fact that Queen Anne shillings might decorate the bowls of punch ladles with hallmarks of George III. (Punch ladles made during the eighteenth century were required by law to be fully hallmarked, and these were usually punched in the bowl). Silver-gilt bowls sometimes incorporated golden guineas or gilded shillings or sixpences. Later examples of punch ladles might be hemispherical with a wide lip above the rim, popularly decorated with chased grapes, vine leaves or floral motifs.

25.   Eighteenth century ladles. (J. H. Bourdon-Smith Ltd.)

Knives   Forks

The steel blades of early English table knives varied in shape but were generally of fine steel, stamped with the bladesmith's mark, most of whom were registered in London or Sheffield. Early examples might have pointed or wedge-shaped ends but after approximately the time of the Restoration (1660) they were rounded, curved or spatulate, and the latter shape was the one which prevailed during the following century. Sometimes a set of six early knives might be kept in a 'canteen', but for many years a knife was a piece of personal equipage and for centuries the knife, with the aid of the spoon, sufficed the needs at table.

Towards the end of the seventeenth century travelling knives and forks became more in evidence and these usually had tapering, cylindrical handles with flat ends. Around the turn of the eighteenth century sets with their handles formed like pistol butts became more general. The green stained ivory handle similarly shaped dates from approximately 1750. Staghorn was also used throughout the eighteenth century. The early years of the Georgian period saw the arrival of the fashion for knives and forks with matching silver handles in various patterns including the pistol butt shape while others might be reeded or plain, or perhaps with a shell adorning the finial. Costs remained high until after about 1775 when the hafts or handles were stamped from thinly rolled silver, enveloping a cheaply produced resinous composition. They were made in vast quantities by Sheffield cutlers. These handles deteriorated with the constant use and atmospheric condition and because of this a complete set of the cheaply produced variety is seldom found in good condition.

Dessert knives with silver blades sometimes with hard stone handles appeared around 1785. Folding fruit knives were also made from the eighteenth century onwards.

Very early forks were thick and straight, either square, round or hexagonal in section. After the Restoration the fork became slowly more general. Gradually the handle became flatter with a trifid end. People continued to carry their own cutlery when they travelled, in an etui, possibly made of shagreen with silver embellishments, and containing a small knife, fork and spoon.

During the eighteenth century the trifid terminal disappeared, evolving into a graceful sweep or curve. The prongs were lengthened and became more in proportion to the handle. Handles of steel-pronged forks were made *en suite* with those of steel knives. Varied decoration appeared on silver forks from about 1765, reflecting the tastes in current fashions (described in Chapter 2). Extremely popular was the fiddle shape with square shoulders, and, later, the opulent king's pattern and more restrained queen's pattern. However, silver was not the only material used for hafts of expensive forks. Many were made in ivory, amber, enamel, tortoiseshell, mother-of-pearl and semi-precious stones like agate and onyx in conjunction with silver mounts. Others might be delicately inlaid with precious metals. Cheaper forks would have handles of wood or bone, their prongs being of steel.

Although matching sets of cutlery were known of towards the end of the seventeenth century, their general use came about very slowly, so that it was not until the beginning of the Georgian period that silver knives and forks with matching handles of cast silver gradually became fashionable among the wealthy (see *Knives*).

General Utensils
Skewers

Very few early silver skewers are extant prior to those made after approximately the fourth decade of the eighteenth century, although wooden skewers (skivers) were used long before this to pin together joints of meat into manageable and presentable shapes. These were probably cut mostly from dogwood until the end of the seventeenth century, when lignum vitae became more generally used.

Early examples of the silver skewer are tapering and rectangular in section, mostly heavy and cut from flat plate. They were produced in sets of varying lengths to cater for different sizes of joints, the smaller ones which were about six or seven inches long, probably destined for game or small cuts. Those of eleven to fifteen inches would be intended for more cumbersome and larger joints.

At one end of the skewer a finial or ring (loop) would project from the meat for ease of handling. By 1790, a sharp-edged skewer, today sometimes used as a paper knife, became general. Other examples were formed similarly to a bodkin, and these are reckoned to be of the earlier form. They have an elongated 'eye' at one end. Finials varied in decoration and design. They included thread and shell, shells, crests and, into the nineteenth century, boar's heads, dolphins and tridents. Skewers were generally hallmarked close to the loop.

Fish Slices

Fish slices are seldom found earlier than about 1770. It is thought that their appearance then was due to the growing penchant for whitebait. At first fish slices were trowel-shaped, with openwork foliated scrolls in varying designs, and, no doubt, they were used for other purposes since they have also been described as pudding trowels in eighteenth century ledgers. One of the finest examples of the original fish slice is by Paul de Lamerie, c.1740 (Ashmolean Museum, Oxford) which has a handle like that of a spoon with a blade shaped as a flat, oval disc which is pierced and engraved with scrolls and fish.

By approximately 1780 the outline of the blade looked roughly like the shape of a fish, sometimes being a firm fish-like silhouette. Piercing was attractive, perhaps around the periphery of the blade, with additional motifs and classical ornament to augment it. A space left unpierced near the handle might be decorated with a monogram or crest of the owner. Handles were commonly of turned ivory, stained green, plain or carved. Around the turn of the nineteenth century, the almost symmetrical blade gave way to the shape of the fish knife in general use today. At about this time a fish slice was supplied with many services of table silver, the handle matching the rest of the flatware.

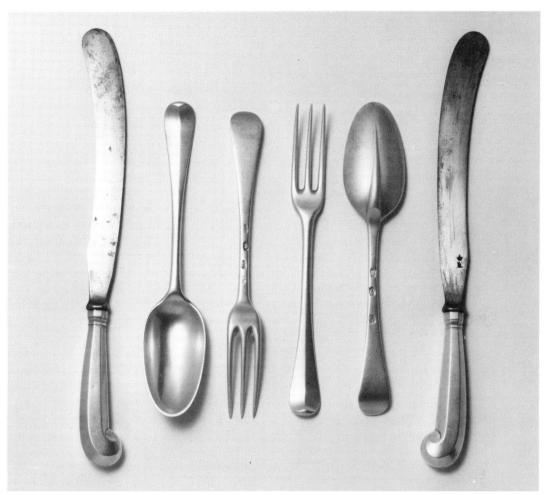

26.　*Knives, spoons and three-pronged forks, c.1713 and c.1714. The steel blades of the knives are stamped with the bladesmith's mark and the handles are formed like pistol butts. (Christie's)*

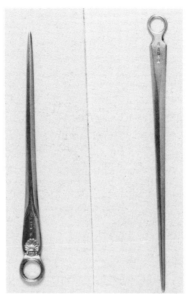

27. Left: thread and shell
     meat skewer, London,
     1841; right: plain meat
     skewer, Exeter, 1818.
     (J. H. Bourdon-Smith
     Ltd.)

Late nineteenth century and early twentieth century fish slices and serving forks of good quality electro-plate are still reasonable in price, useful in the home and handsome upon the table. Some are decorated, others are plain and if you are lucky you may find those with sterling silver ferrules at the joint of the blade and the handle, in which case the ferrules should be hallmarked.

Grape Shears (Scissors)

These mostly date from about 1800, although a scant number made during the late eighteenth century is in existence. Early examples are unadorned with simple ring handles, the blades resembling sewing scissors. Later, the blades became more efficient when they were made in a secateur-shape. This improvement meant that the comparatively soft silver remained sharper for a longer period. Decoration of later examples complemented the purpose of the shears being based on grapes and vine foliage. Opulent canteens of cutlery sometimes contained two pairs of ornate grape shears.

Marrow Scoops

At one time the marrow scoop was a vital and useful utensil in England. Changing habits and tastes have rendered it redundant in this country. Marrow scoops are

28.   Eighteenth century slices. (Phillips)

quite common. They were used for the simple purpose of scooping the marrow from cooked marrow bones. They were usually formed with two scoops, one at either end, one of which would be smaller, intended for more inaccessible regions of the bone. The slender length of silver between the scoops was rarely decorated. Marrow scoops emerged during the early years of the eighteenth century and grew increasingly popular, so that by the end of the century they had become a very general utensil. Eighteenth century knife boxes often had a place for marrow scoops.

Sugar Tongs and Sugar Nippers

Sugar tongs are particularly amenable little items to collect since, not only are many of them beautiful, but they are also easily housed and their function is still appropriate in the modern home. However, watch out for repaired bow-shaped tongs. The hallmarks of these will often have become obscured during the soldering.

Sugar tongs evolved from early sugar nippers, the shape of which resembled contemporary fire tongs, no doubt since it was logical to copy another domestic utensil which performed a similar function, even though this was on a larger scale. The earliest of these, c.1685 preceeded by far later examples which consisted of baluster-turned arms terminating in oval, circular or shell pans. Around 1700 the spring bow was succeeded by a spring hinge incorporated into the bow and within about fifteen years a scissor-shaped nipper appeared. These were usually given large, circular handles and scrolled stems, their pans often in the form of shells or scrolls. One form which was copied during the nineteenth century was that of the stork, which was hinged through the eye, the claws at the end of the legs shaped like pans and the body chased with feathers.

The bow-shaped sugar tong, generally in use today, first appeared in the 1760's, becoming increasingly more popular until it eventually supplanted the scissor type after about 1775. Bow-shaped tongs were made simply, in three parts with cast, pierced arms and a plain bow. These parts were then joined together by solder, the bow having first been hammered to produce a springy quality. Later they were made entirely from one piece of metal, the bow being slightly curved in section to give it the necessary degree of tensibility. Bow-shaped tongs of the last twenty-five years or so of the eighteenth century have great charm, often being beautifully decorated in the idiom of the day, delicately engraved and bright cut. They are well able to hold their own with the ornate pierced examples. Such delightful embellishment disappeared later and by the turn of the nineteenth century many tongs were given fiddle-shaped spoon grips, were left undecorated or were only sparsely ornamented. They were larger than their predecessors. The smaller, more fragile sugar tongs made concurrently with the plain variety during the nineteenth century were usually sold en suite with silver sugar bowls, while their heavy, plain contemporaries with longer arms were produced to accompany the large ceramic sugar bowls in fashion at that time. Scissor-shaped tongs were also available and had cast foliate motifs. They were sometimes of silver-gilt.

CHAPTER 5

Tea Silver

Teapots

It is hard to imagine an English home without a teapot, yet it was not until the early eighteenth century that tea grew in popularity as a national beverage, despite the fact that it was known of far earlier. In September 1660, Samuel Pepys entered in his diary, "I did send for a cup of tee (a China drink) of which I never had drunk before".

Within ten years the East India Company started to import tea in a small quantity and in 1678 tea became an import of substance. The total weight was 4,713 pounds. By 1700 this had increased to 20,000 pounds and within twenty-one years it was more than 1,000,000 pounds.

There was certainly a need for some sort of pot in which to infuse the beverage for which this newly acquired taste was rapidly spreading. However, at first this vessel was a peculiar, crude looking object which stood 13½ inches high (see Chapter I). One would be left unsure as to its purpose, assuming it to be for coffee, were it not for the inscription engraved upon it: "this silver tea pott was presented to ye comm^tte of ye East India Company . . . 1670" It is engraved with the Arms of the East India Company and Lord Berkeley. (Victoria and Albert Museum).

One of the earliest vessels to resemble a normal teapot was melon-shaped and made by Charles Shelley. It appeared before about 1679. This had a narrow, recurving spout and a wooden handle pinned into two silver sockets. Two gilt examples of approximately 1685 are in the Victoria and Albert Museum and the Ashmolean Museum, Oxford.

When Queen Anne ascended the throne in 1702 tea drinking was a well-established ritual among the wealthy of the land who poured this expensive beverage from dainty pear-shaped teapots, octagonal or round, their curving spouts perhaps culminating in the shape of a bird's head (variously described as duck, goose or swan). These little teapots might be plain or perhaps decorated by Huguenot silversmiths with applied cut-card work (see Chapter 2). They were generally no more than about six inches tall, had a hinged, domed cover with a finial of metal or a wooden knop and simple wooden handles, perhaps curved, plain or covered in leather, pinned into circular sockets. Sometimes the spout had a small, hinged lid at its end, and on early examples this was attached by a short chain. These charming teapots remained in fashion for approximately the first twenty-five years of the eighteenth century.

29. *Pear-shaped teapot, Exeter, 1718. (Garrard and Company Ltd.)*

During the 1720's, a shape that can be described as relatively modern in appearance became increasingly popular. This was global or bullet-shaped and a very early example had been made by Anthony Nelme in 1712. Eventually the global pot replaced altogether the pear-shaped variety. It had a narrow, moulded ring base and its lid generally fitted flush into its flattish top. Handles were usually of wood, but the spouts were straight (unlike those of pear-shaped pots). Scottish teapots of this kind were far more spherical than those made in England, and they had a stemmed foot in most cases.

By the 1730's the English teapot, in common with other pieces of domestic silver came under the influence of the rococo style. Not all teapots conformed to this, but those that did might have spouts shaped like dragons and were decorated by floral designs intermingled with C and S scrolls. Cover finials took on the form of the ubiquitious pineapple or Chinaman. The Chinaman was typical of a contemporanious style of decoration which was a robust, vigorous form of *chinoiseries,* a simple version of which had been popular during the latter years of the seventeenth century. Towards the middle of the eighteenth century an inverted pear-shape pot emerged. It stood upon a short stem with a wide foot-rim and decoration might include flat-chased borders or embossed rococo embellishments. Spouts were curved and sometimes fluted in the swan-neck farm. Handles were often double scrolls with pleasant fluid lines.

Despite the high cost of tea its popularity continued to spread, even the boys at Eton had a penchant for the beverage. In Maxwell Lyte's *History of Eton,* a pupil wrote to his father in 1766 saying, "I wish you would be so kind as to let me have Tea and Sugar here to drink in the afternoon, without which there is no such thing as keeping company with other boys of my standing". With the increase in demand for tea came the need for more teapots, but until this time those made in silver were costly, generally hammered up from the flat from heavy-gauge silver. Now, however, two important factors were to greatly lessen the cost of producing the teapot and all other pieces of domestic silver. One was the dawn of the neo-classical period and its easily produced straight-sided teapots, which practically coincided with the technical progress resulting in less expensive, thinly-rolled silver, which was ideal for such teapots.

Neo-classical teapots might be circular, oval or polygonal in shape with flat bases and vertical sides. Decoration included vertical or spiral palmettes, acanthus leaves, shallow fluting, *paterae,* rams' heads, the key pattern, running floral S scrolls, laurel wreaths, swags of foliage or cloth and ribbon bows. The result was an elegant vessel, exquisitely decorated.

Because of the flat base of the neo-classical teapot and the corresponding tendency to mark tables, a silver stand would often be placed beneath it which had four moulded feet. By the turn of the nineteenth century, however, the stand had given way to the four moulded feet being incorporated in the base of the pot.

Towards the final years of the eighteenth century the graceful, beautifully proportioned teapots of the neo-classical era were already being overshadowed by the heavy opulence which emerged during the nineteenth century. Designs were numerous during the Regency period and successive years. Teapots might be

30.   Teapot by Francis Crump, London, 1772. (S. J. Shrubsole Ltd.)

square, polygonal, oval or circular, their sides usually curving upwards and outwards to an angular shoulder, above which the incurved necks were surmounted by a domed cover. The general shape of many was of a square, oval form. One popular design had a peaked front.

The shapes of Victorian teapots were as diverse as the patterns and styles which were borrowed during the nineteenth century from preceding designs. They were often encrusted by heavy ornament (see Chapter 2) and were mostly the very opposite to their eighteenth century counterparts. Certainly they took on a confusing assortment of shapes, some echoing faintly the lines of the eighteenth century neo-classical period, while others possessed a strange ecclesiastical quality derived from a Gothic influence. At the International Exhibition of 1862 there were, among others, tea and coffee services in the Greek style with urn-shaped vessels, decorated by fluting, the key design or ovolo borders; those in the Renaissance style adorned with scrolls and rock motifs; and Elizabethan-style teapots with strapwork and cartouches, to say nothing of other peculiar styles resulting from 'marriages' of shapes and decoration.

Few exaggerated Victorian teapots would complement today's homes, but

70

31.   Five-piece tea and coffee set by R. & S. Hennell, 1809-10. (Sotheby)

among those which would are the more or less straight-forward copies of the neo-classical teapot. Collectors who have their sights set on a complete service, however, will have to take their choice from the very late eighteenth century or nineteenth century and later, since it was not until the last years of the former century that services began to appear in any number. They usually consisted of a teapot, milk jug, sugar bowl and hot water jug. Nineteenth century services commonly included a coffee pot.

Early examples of teapots generally have hallmarks punched in a line near the top of the body below the rim near the handle. After about 1760 they were usually punched on the base of the pot. When the lid is hallmarked, make sure that what is there matches corresponding marks on other parts of the pot. Also, when looking for an eighteenth century neo-classical example with a silver stand, do not worry if the two pieces do not match because they were often sold separately.

Sugar Boxes, Bowls and Baskets

Sugar containers in silver are unlikely to have been made before the sixteenth century, and then probably as an accompaniment to the wine service. However, as sugar became more widely consumed so a gradually increasing number of sugar boxes appeared. Inventories of the seventeenth century sometimes refer to such objects as being accompanied by a sugar box spoon. These boxes were shallow, perhaps scallop shaped and with a hinged lid. They stood upon four pretty feet formed as shells. Others might be circular and lobed or left plain. They were often very beautiful, and in all probability were used to contain other palatable goodies apart from sugar.

By the last ten years or so of the seventeenth century, sugar bowls with loose covers were becoming fashionable. They were very similar to the imported covered bowls of Chinese porcelain. The silver counterpart was hemispherical and about six inches wide, standing upon an applied moulded foot ring. The cover incorporated a circular shape at its summit, so that when it was removed from the bowl it could be inverted and stood upon this circular 'base'. It is thought that the cover would then have been used for a dish upon which to place tea spoons, since saucers supplied another need – tea was sipped from the saucer at that time and thus there was nowhere to place the spoon. Small trays for tea spoons were also made for this purpose, although during approximately the last third of the eighteenth century these fell into disuse, probably indicating changes in the habit of tea drinking.

During the 1730's the sugar bowl became more decorative. It was larger and embellished with low chasing or engraving, perhaps with a cartouche for a crest or initials. Gradually during the following thirty years or so the bowl shape altered, first taking on an ogee form with a deep, ringed cover and then becoming an attractive vase form, containing a blue flint glass line, the cover ring giving way to a more decorative finial, perhaps a pineapple. The external silver would be all-over embossed.

Like other items used at the tea table, the sugar bowl benefited in design from the neo-classical influence. Bowls now began to appear in various graceful shapes, many of which did not incorporate a cover. Fashionable during the 1770's was a far more elegant vase shape which tapered to its perfectly proportioned stem above a circular foot. Two small handles either side of the shoulders might be linked by decorative swags and bows. A domed cover with an ornamental finial completed the shape.

Pierced ornament was much favoured during the neo-classical period. The upper part of the bowl might be delicately pierced with geometric patterns and embossed with festoons to complement the lower, solid portion which might be decorated with an elongated foliate design, stretching upward from the stem. The cover of this type of container would be decorated to match the bottom half of the vase-shaped bowl, which continued to be popular until the first decade or so of the nineteenth century. This design, and those which were similar, were also made of unpierced silver and decorated with the usual type of neo-classical motifs (see Chapter 2).

Popular indeed was the neo-classical boat-shaped sugar basket. It has been copied extensively by successive generations. It appeared during roughly the last two decades of the eighteenth century, taking the form of an elliptical 'boat', standing upon a short stem and foot ring. It might be either pierced or solid. It was beautifully decorated with festoons, bows or other appropriate classical

72

32.   Silver-gilt tea and coffee set by E. Fernell, London 1816-18. (M.P. Levene Ltd.)

motifs, usually engraved or bright-cut, with swing handles. Small wonder that they graced so many tables and have continued to do so ever since.

Not so graceful were other shapes made during the final years of the eighteenth century and later which included the oval form with a flat base, commonly included in the tea services of the day and echoing the form of the teapot of that period. The sugar bowl, as with the teapot, might be raised upon four ball-shaped feet, which later expanded, became more elaborate and were integrated into the main design of the piece. By the second decade of the nineteenth century a melon-shaped bowl with over-all embossing and scroll handles appeared . Later Victorian examples followed the exaggerated styles then in fashion.

Apart from the sugar containers already mentioned, there were those produced during the eighteenth century which were intended to be kept in tea chests. Originally the tea chest held only tea canisters but towards approximately the 1750's a silver sugar box would often be included. This would naturally match the

33. *Late eighteenth century pierced sugar basket with beaded handle. (S. J. Shrubsole Ltd.)*

accompanying tea canisters but was often a little larger. It was succeeded by a flint glass bowl.

Another form of container was the small sugar bucket, commonly pierced, which might partner a solid-sided pail intended for cream. Both had swing handles. The sugar bucket would have a glass liner.

Milk Jugs

Milk taken with tea does not seem to have become general until the eighteenth century. Samuel Pepys referred to his cup of tea as 'clear and unspoiled'. However, Matthew Prior, the poet, in his poem To a Young Gentleman in Love which he wrote in 1720, declares, "He thanked her on his bended knee; then drank a quart of milk and tea". Presumably by then milk and tea were irrevocably linked.

No earlier examples of milk jugs ('milk potts') than those made during the reign of Queen Anne are known to be recorded. Early uncovered milk jugs were tiny. Sometimes they might be only about three inches in height. They were roughly pear shaped, rotund and fairly squat, not unlike an early beer jug. They were generally made from four sections of cast silver: the main body, an open spout, a narrow moulded foot-ring and a plain scroll handle usually with a small thumb piece on top. As with certain other early vessels of this era, the handle and spout were at right angles to each other. After about the first decade of the eighteenth century these small jugs were sometimes eight or six sided. Also at this time a covered jug was made, of similar shape, with wood or ivory handles and with lip spouts, and it is thought that these were intended for hot milk which was also served with tea.

Towards the 1730's another shape emerged which was very similar to an inverted helmet. This was comparatively graceful and the form was probably derived from the water ewers which were made in the same style. It was made from a single sheet of silver, carefully shaped to incorporate the broad lip. The handle was cast and soldered to the main body. Although it stood upon a spreading moulded foot, a new idea was also introduced to balance the helmet shape. Three cast feet were used and these became so popular that they shortly supported the body of the pear-shaped jug, transforming its rotund, basic outline into one of more elegance, the tiny legs ending in scroll feet to complete the transformation. Although most of these jugs were undecorated, there were those which were elaborately ornate with rococo adornment, embossed and chased with flowers and landscapes, perhaps hunting or sporting scenes spreading over the jug. Scrolls and shells abounded on others.

Worthy of mention are the handles of jugs. They can sometimes be a rough guide to the age. These generally became more decorative towards the middle of the eighteenth century. The ordinary C and S scrolled handles of earlier jugs were thus succeeded by more intricate examples, sometimes embellished by gadrooning, reeding or beading. Perhaps a chased acanthus leaf might be placed at the top of the handle. In other cases this might be left as a simple, flat thumb rest. Some handles, curved and recurved quite extensively, terminating at the top in a decorative mould (the mask of a ram, exotic bird or other contemporary motif), or at the bottom curve perhaps in a volute tail. Legs, too, were decorated, and as with the furniture of the period, they might have feet shaped as hoofs, paws (sometimes the plain Dutch pad), the joint of the leg to the main body being decorated with animal masks, shells or other suitable ornament.

Of contrast to such decoration was another type of jug with definite pastoral origins, and not particularly attractive except in a primitive or novelty way. This was the milk jug which was formed like a cow, made in sections and soldered together. Originally thought to be of Dutch origin, most of these were made by John Schuppe who registered his mark in 1753. The jug was filled on top of the body through an opening with a hinged lid, sometimes this had a border of engraved flowers and leaves, its knob for raising the lid being formed as a fly. The milk was poured from the cow's mouth and the jug held by a handle shaped like the animal's tail. Silver cow jugs have been emulated over the years, but most lack the craftsmanship of the original Schuppe jugs.

Neo-classical jugs embraced the usual classical outlines of the period. They were commonly octagonal on plan, tapering gracefully from rim to base with a slender stem joining the main body to the foot, circular or oval, perhaps mounted upon a four-sided plinth. Decoration was mainly by engraving, and later bright-cutting. The handle, too, had its own degree of elegance, rising from the rim, recurving then sweeping down to the base in a graceful outline. Many of these jugs were produced in very thin silver and were generally made in two parts, the foot produced as a separate item.

By the last few years of the eighteenth century another shape of jug was also current. It had a broad oval body on a flat base. When the nineteenth century dawned, many jugs were raised upon four ball-shaped feet which later became ornate.

Nineteenth century jugs for the tea table were many and varied, based often on preceeding styles but usually not well proportioned or appropriately decorated. Some were in the form of a Roman urn, the lower half of the body gadrooned or reeded, others were decorated lavishly with naturalistic ornament, or in the Elizabethan style with heavy strapwork. Gothic, Louis Quatorze or Louis Quinze with C and S scrolls and flower and foliate patterns were the styles of others. In design they were far removed from the prosaic little jug of the early eighteenth century. Yet by the end of the nineteenth century such simplicity was to be restored in some degree by members of the School and Guild of Handicraft (see Chapter 2) and thus design was to make a full revolution.

Tea Canisters and Caddies

Tea drinkers throughout the world know the necessity of keeping tea in the right conditions so that it will not deteriorate and lose its subtle flavour. When tea was first introduced to England the problem was new. No canisters or caddies existed. There was also a further factor of importance to be considered which was the high

34.   *Milk jugs, top, left to right: 1802, 1763, 1825; below, left to right: 1797, 1788,*
1792. (J. H. Bourdon-Smith Ltd.)

cost of tea. Because of the latter the early tea canister was diminutive, perhaps
only a mere three inches in height, and probably based on the shape of certain
imported oriental porcelain jars. This shape was simple, the sides rose straight
from a rectangular base, curved in at the shoulders to a circular neck, which was
fitted with a separate domed cover. In some later examples, the top section slid
off, while others had a sliding panel fitted in the base. An early canister c.1699 at
the Ashmolean Museum is 3⅛ inches high with panels on each side and a circular
slip-on cap.

By the first two decades of the eighteenth century the canister had grown in
height and was rectangular, octagonal or hexagonal, occasionally triangular. It
stood on a moulded base and its cover by now might have a hinge. The dome-and-
neck canister was made until after the middle of the eighteenth century, running
concurrently with other similar designs, in particular a rectangular box shape
with a stepped lid to complement, or to match, the applied foot-rim which was
built in tiers of moulding. A further shape, particularly attractive, was based on

35.   Queen Anne tea canister by Thomas Ash, 1710. (J. H. Bourdon-Smith Ltd.)

36. *Magnificent and rare set of tea canisters and chest (mother-of-pearl with silver mounts) with pierced tea spoons, mote skimmer and sugar tongs by Edward Darville, London, 1762. (Spink and Son Ltd.)*

an oriental type of vase and decorated with floral designs and flowing scrolls. More opulent was the bombé-shaped canister, derived from furniture of the period, particularly commodes, which appeared around the middle of the century. This might stand upon a base rim or have small feet daintily shaped, perhaps as acanthus leaves. The cover was slightly domed and had a finial in the form of a pineapple, shell or Chinaman.

Tea canisters of the earlier type might be produced as single pieces, but by the 1730's a new fashion required that they should be made in sets and contained in an outer box – a chest – usually of wood, or wood covered with shagreen, sometimes mother-of-pearl or tortoiseshell. These might contain either three canisters (for different types of tea), or, later, two canisters for tea and a sugar container. The chest or case might have ornamental silver mounts and key plate because tea was still expensive and kept securely locked. The idea of locking away tea persisted into the nineteenth century, even through the price was by then more realistic.

Canisters made during the neo-classical period were far larger than their small predecessors and often held more than twice the amount contained in the dome-and-neck type. The emergence of new and less costly silver manufacturing techniques meant that these could be sold to an increasing public at a more reasonable cost. In common with the other pieces of tea equipage was the very fashionable vase or urn shape. The flowing, tapering body might be embossed in low relief with a variety of Adam-style motifs and radiating convex fluting. The elegant, incurving shoulders met a domed cover. The whole stood upon a slender stem and concave foot. There might be a square platform or plinth at the base. Sometimes loop, ring or (later) taller handles were added.

Another shape fashionable at the same time was the box canister. This might be square, rectangular or hexagonal, often beautifully decorated by bright-cut or engraved neo-classical motifs. A decorative finial would surmount the flat top. Usually covers were hinged, so that they could be locked. Sometimes decoration would take the form of Chinese characters. Popular, also, was the oval box, often fluted with a raised lid. During the Regency period this shape might be embossed with various decoration including a tea plantation, perhaps combining Adam motifs with embossed *chinoiseries.*

Neo-classical and earlier tea canisters are expensive. However, many canisters were also made in Sheffield plate, and since these emulated the styles which were fashionable in silver, collectors may find an example which is not too badly worn. The canister was not know as a caddy until the end of the eighteenth century. The word is said to have orginated from *kati,* a Malay weight, equal to a little over one pound avoirdupois.

CHAPTER 6

Silver and The Table

Collectors may indulge themselves no end when it comes to general table silver, since everything can be of practical use in the home today. Naturally, this does not embrace rare or fragile objects, but many of the pieces mentioned in this chapter are as functional today as they were when they were first made.

Mustard Pots

These are certainly as useful today as they ever were. Mustard has been known of since earliest times. It can be traced back as far as 3000 BC in India, and both the ancient Greeks and Romans were acquainted with it. In the great medieval houses, mustard was used with a wide variety of foods including meat and fish, the job of mustarder becoming common by the thirteenth century. Professional saucemakers used querns to pound the seed and smaller domestic versions became available for the home.

Although John Wycliffe was known to keep a pot of mustard ready mixed as early as 1380, it was not until the 1720's that mustard pots made a real appearance, since mustard was also popular sprinkled dry. Mustard pots followed the arrival of the production of mustard on a commercial scale, for which we must thank an enterprising lady called Mrs. Clements who started making mustard flour in about 1720 from 73 Saddler Street, Durham. Her simple method was to grind the seed in a mill and then to process it as ordinary flour. This mustard flour found quick success and soon became a popular relish. In 1742 Messrs. Keens established a mustard-making factory at Garlick Hill, London. Their methods of producing mustard were similar to those used by Colmans, by whom they were acquired in 1903. Colmans started in the business in 1814.

Originally, dry mustard was sprinkled over the food from a caster. When prepared mustard became more popular and the pierced holes of the caster were no longer necessary, these were blocked by the insertion of a 'sleeve' and the resulting caster is described as a 'blind' mustard. However, although mustard pots appeared after Mrs. Clements introduced her mustard flour, they did not become greatly fashionable until approximately the 1750's, since the 'blind' mustard was used instead.

From the early 1760's, silversmiths described small tankards with flat hinged lids which were cut with an aperture for a spoon, as mustard tankards. They were known of before this time, however, drum-shaped or cylindrical and sometimes

38. *A straight-sided oval mustard pot, bright-cut with festoons and borders by Charles Chesterman II, London, 1788. (The Colman Collection)*

37. *Facing Page: A 'blind' mustard on a low moulded foot by Edward Gibbon, London, 1724. (The Colman Collection)*

oval or octagonal. The body of the tankard was made from a sheet of silver, joined by a soldered seam beneath the handle. The lid was raised by a thumbpiece which was cast and chased, pierced or shell-shaped, and which hinged backwards over a scroll or S-shaped handle. The solid base was later changed to openwork so that the glass liner which contained the mustard might be removed by pushing up from beneath.

Neo-classical forms included the vase-shaped pot and the elliptical shape. Piercing was extremely fashionable and often beautiful. By the early 1780's vase-shaped mustards on pedestal feet were pierced and engraved with geometric designs and classical motifs, perhaps edged with beading, their domed lids topped be a cast or turned decorative finial. This period produced a great diversity of mustard pot design, since new advances in techniques now meant that a wide variety of pierced patterns could be achieved by mechanical methods. Originally pierced examples were worked by hand, but with the introduction of the fly-press such skilled work was no longer necessary and mass production replaced it in general. Bright-cutting and engraving were used to enhance these neo-classical mustard pots, which also included a cylindrical shape with either a flat or domed lid.

Towards the final years of the eighteenth century, straight-sided oval mustard pots appeared, decorated by engraving, bright-cutting and beading, as with the other shapes. They held as much as the cylindrical pot, although they were shorter. Rectangular pots, seldom pierced, also appeared at about this time, and the barrel-shaped pot followed around the turn of the century.

Regency mustard pots were made in the varying styles prevalent at the time, but did not show any great distinction of their own, probably because the silver cruet frame was now fashionable, incorporating as a matter of course a silver mounted mustard pot, together with its other containers. During the 1820's, fashion dictated a revival of rococo which continued for many years, being joined and succeeded in their turn by naturalism and the many flamboyant and opulent styles of the nineteenth century. New shapes included a compressed circular form chased with naturalistic ornament and the pear-shaped pot. Hexagonal or octagonal pots were pierced or engraved.

Novelty ideas captured the imagination of a receptive public during the 1860's and 1870's. Mustard pots emerged under numerous guises including Punch and Judy, owls, monkeys, cats, dogs, the heads of babies and also clowns. By the final two decades or so of the nineteenth century, shapes were geared to mass-production and surfaces were mechanically smoothed and polished. Decoration was usually rather uninspired. *Art nouveau* designs which followed were fluid and artistically opposed to the welter of mass-produced pots, but *art nouveau* was not very long-lived and mustard pots in general continued to be functional and ordinary.

39.   *Facing Page: A novelty mustard pot, cast and chased in the form of a busby by Elkington & Co. Ltd., London, 1908. (The Colman Collection)*

Sugar Casters, Pepper Casters, Flour Dredgers and Muffineers

Casters have long played an important role at the table, namely for pepper, dry mustard and sugar. Highly spiced food was popular from Elizabethan days and pepper was sold in large quantities, yet it was not until the Restoration in 1660 that casters, in common with other pieces of silver grew more numerous.

Casters were generally made singly or in sets of three, one large for sugar and two small for Jamaican, cayenne peppers or dry mustard. Among the earliest extant examples is one owned by the Victoria and Albert Museum c.1658 and two which belong to Queen's College, Oxford, c.1670. They stand approximately five inches high. These early casters were usually cylindrical with straight, vertical sides, perhaps fluted. Body and cover were secured by a bayonet joint and the cover was pierced with simple foliate and geometrical piercings. The cylindrical shape was general until the late seventeenth century when a rounded dome cover appeared which was a little smaller in diameter than the body. Its piercing was more skilful and elaborate than previous casters.

By the beginning of the eighteenth century a pear-shaped caster was emerging, standing on a moulded foot, and similar in shape (as with other items of domestic silver) to imported oriental vases of the period. Others remained straight sided or octagonal and baluster in form. Earlier casters were generally sparsely decorated, except perhaps for a horizontal band of moulding. They were later more ornate, sometimes with a decorative cartouche. From approximately 1750 the 'dropped bottom' appeared, that is the hemispherical lower section of the pear-shaped body was lowered, not uncommonly with narrow bands of gadrooning around the rim of the cover, the shoulder of the body and the foot. The piercing of the cover might follow a lavish spiralling pattern, topped by a spiral finial. The body of the caster would follow a similar decorative theme. The covers of other casters might alternate in narrow diagonal panels with geometric and curved patterns.

The cylindrical shape returned to fashion during the reign of George III, but with a difference, the cover was then pierced in the neo-classical style. At this time, small cylindrical casters were also being made in sets of six or more. There were as well those with pierced sides and blue-glass liners. Earlier designs included pales and arches intermingled with festooned drapery and chased with borders of lace-work. Later the pierced sides were decorated with applied festoons or similar classical-inspired motifs.

From approximately the last decade of the eighteenth century, vase-shaped casters were made prolifically in London, Birmingham and Sheffield. They became more common during the following three decades or so, and were produced alongside casters which echoed the designs of preceding periods, since after about 1800 no new form of sugar caster appears to have been recorded. The Victorians either embellished in their idiom the older casters they possessed, or emulated designs and decoration.

40. Facing Page: Eighteenth century casters. (J. H. Bourdon-Smith Ltd.)

In addition to the casters already mentioned, there was as well another version which had been made from about the last decade of the seventeenth century, and which looked like a tiny flour dredger. The specific use of this remains a little hazy, but it is thought that this form was used as a spice dredger. It stood about four inches high, had a bun-shaped cover with simple perforated holes, and might be cylindrical or octagonal in shape. It incorporated a handle.

A small caster which was in use towards the end of the eighteenth century, when it was usual to sprinkle cinnamon on hot buttered muffins, was known simply as a muffineer. It differed from the spice dredger because it had no handle and was far more elegant, although it was about the same height. It was usually vase-shaped with a low-domed cover which had small circular holes. Eighteenth century examples might be decorated but later muffineers were generally plain. There were also those with pierced sides in the neo-classical style and containing blue-glass liners.

Among the shapes of casters fashionable towards the end of the nineteenth century, was once again the straight-sided cylindrical caster, sometimes with heavily embossed sides and an elaborately pierced cover, as in the case of those being sold by Mappin and Webb at that time; or, following in the tradition of the School and Guild of Handicraft, there were those beautifully hand-worked by C. R. Ashbee and his contemporaries.

Salt Cellars

The basic trencher salt which came into use during the seventeenth century was quickly superseded by more elegant designs after about the third decade of the eighteenth century, and it is these which have been more or less slavishly copied in silver, Sheffield plate and electro-plate ever since. The cauldron shape which appeared in about 1730 usually had three feet, generally shaped as hoofs or scallops, the tiny legs curving neatly into the bowl, sometimes foliated at the junction, or decorated at that point with rams' heads, lions' heads, cherubs and other embellishments. They were made generally in sets of four, the number usually being even, although it is fairly unusual to find sets of more than four with Georgian hallmarks. Linking the decorative joints might be embossed swags or festoons.

From approximately 1760, salt cellars with open-work sides became popular. They contained blue-glass liners to hold the salt and thus helped to prevent the salt from coming into contact with the silver, upon which it has a corrosive effect. The blue of the glass, often in delightful shades, set the silver off to perfection. At first the open-work was cut by hand with the fret-saw (as in all other cases of domestic silver at that time), but by 1770 the fly-press was in use for geometric patterns and scrolls, making such work a viable commercial proposition. Among other manufacturers, Matthew Boulton of Birmingham produced a vast quantity of the pierced bowls used for salt cellars at this time, which were then bought by silversmiths and made into the finished product.

A particularly elegant design and one which found much favour was the

41.   *Top: a pair of cast shell salts by Joseph and John Angell, London, 1834
and a pepperette by Storey and Elliot, London, 1810; below, left to
right: Charles Fox vase-shaped long necked pepperette made in 1839 (its
pair at the other end), a helmet-shaped pepperette by George Unite,
Birmingham, 1878; a dog Toby pepperette by Robert Hennell, London,
1868. (J. H. Bourdon-Smith Ltd.)*

boat-shaped cellar (c1770–1825), with a short stem upon an oval spreading foot.
It looked a little like an Adam tureen in shape. The handles varied. Sometimes a
swing handle of twisted wire was used, while on other examples (usually from
c.1780) high loop handles rose above the rim, starting from just above the stem.

Regency and later nineteenth century salt cellars were made in a miscellany of shapes, and were usually very light in weight. Some were direct copies of the styles already discussed or derived from these designs. The cauldron style on three feet maintained a revived popularity, while others included a bombé shape, a small basket type and those with strong rococo decoration, perhaps with children on rocks holding shells or donkeys with pannier salt holders.

Cruet Frames

The cruet frame was a sensible idea, born out of necessity. Gradually it blossomed and grew in beauty as advances in techniques made this possible. Very early examples are rare, and although they made their appearance around the end of the seventeenth century, most extant examples date from approximately the first few years of the eighteenth century. At first they held only two glass bottles (silver mounted) for oil and vinegar, standing upon a flat, shaped base supported on scroll feet, which held the open framework to contain the bottles. George Ravenscroft had invented flint glass during 1676 and by the following year he was advertising 'diamond cruets' – long-necked bottles with the glass in a raised diamond pattern. The silversmith found an answer for ease of carrying and handing the bottles at table by providing a silver frame to hold them.

The two-bottle cruet frame became more elaborate after about the first two decades of the eighteenth century, emerging as an object of beauty, with attractive pierced galleries. The base of each section might be pierced to match the gallery. A vertical ring handle was positioned between the two sections. The bottles, too, were splendid, their silver caps now finely decorated and perhaps fitted with a spout. A domed, hinged cover completed the design. Handles were double-scrolled.

A boat-shaped tray became fashionable from around c.1770, its graceful base terminating each end in scrolls, which matched the dainty scrolled feet. The base at this time was hardly decorated, but might incorporate beading at the edge of the tray. The handle in the centre was also plain, although by the nineteenth century it had become most ornate. Other shapes included square, oval, oblong or circular, where appropriate with cut corners. There were so many alternatives that a manufacturer might have several hundred versions in his catalogues, spanning a period from the latter years of the eighteenth century and into the first years of the following century.

When sugar, pepper and dry mustard casters were also included in the frame together with the oil and vinegar containers, these were termed Warwick cruets (c.1759), it is thought after the Earl of Warwick. (The Warwick Cruet, 1715, had five silver casters).

Larger cruet frames were made from approximately the middle of the eighteenth century. They might contain three silver mounted glass bottles instead of two, the extra one being for soy sauce. These more commodious frames maintained their popularity into the nineteenth century, when a soy frame often held as many as ten bottles for numerous sauces.

42.   Cruet by Huguenot silversmith Pezé Pilleau, 1731.

From around 1765 there was a short period during which silver casters and glass oil and vinegar bottles were replaced by containers made of the new white enamel glass, embellished with designs in coloured enamels. These were silver mounted. It is thought that the success of the white enamelled glass in the cruet frame, which coincided with improvements in clear flint glass and its attraction when deeply cut, lead to the abandonment of all-silver casters and their subsequent replacement by silver-mounted glass containers. These less costly cruets became extremely popular which accounted for the amazing diversity in their design.

Nineteenth-century cruet sets followed the styles in general of the day. Less costly examples might consist merely of platforms with rococo borders and feet

with four matching supports. Towards the middle of the nineteenth century and later, simplified two-bottle and three-bottle soy frames were made.

When buying a cruet frame it is important, if they are to be an investment, that they hold their original bottles. The glass in very early bottles had striations and small bubbles. By about 1750 flint-glass contained less lead and was whiter and lighter in weight, but it still lacked prismatic 'fire'. This became apparent only after about 1800 with advances in technical processes. A vast number of cruet frames was also produced in Sheffield plate, and these followed the styles of those in silver.

Sauce Boats and Sauce Tureens

Sauce boats are another eighteenth century refinement at the table. The first examples date from about the early twenties, and live up to the name which was given them, since they very much resembled a boat with a pouring lip at each end and decorative scrolled handles on opposite sides. They had attractive wavy rims which looked pleasing, but must have caused many an embarrassed scene at table, since the contents must have flowed from the rim in addition to the lip when the sauce boat was held at a certain angle. This double-lipped example was used until approximately the 1730's, but from about 1726 a single-lipped sauce boat with a scroll handle appeared. Within another decade the moulded base was superseded by three or four decorative cast feet, masks, shells and claws among the shapes which predominated. The boat outline became more oval and a further design also emerged. This was the bombé form which resembled a bombé shaped tureen, incorporating a curved pouring lip on the opposite end to a cast handle composed of scrolls. Decoration on the body of the tureen was either minimal or vigorously embossed with rococo ornament.

A more opulent version which was made in the forties and fifties had a rounded bowl, sometimes fluted, with an ornamental shaped rim. It stood upon a short stem with a spreading foot, decorated in the rococo style. The cast handle, opposite the lip, was sometimes extravagantly formed as an animal's or bird's head. During the mid-eighteenth century and the following decade certain sauce tureens were small and matching editions of the bombé tureens which was used with them. From the last quarter of the eighteenth century many dinner services included four or more sauce tureens.

Neo-classical styles were superbly proportioned and popularly of oval form, standing upon a spreading stem and broad base, with sweeping, high loop handles. Body decoration for the most part consisted of swags of husks or bay

43. *Facing Page: A magnificent, rare, silver-gilt coffee pot on a stand with a lamp by IRH, London, 1850, lavishly decorated in the manner of Teniers. (Spink and Son Ltd.)*

wreaths, looped over *paterae*. The edges were usually beaded, reeded or gadrooned, and the cover likewise decorated with fluting or gadrooning as was the stem or base. Regency styles continued to match the remainder of the dinner service, sometimes florid, often upon four cast feet, while others might be fairly plain. The Victorian sauce boat generally fell into the latter category, with rotund sides and a gadrooned rim which was sometimes scalloped. Handles might be formed as double scrolls and the boat stood upon three hoof feet. They were made in three sizes, when sold singly.

Coffee Pots

By the early eighteenth century the coffee pot was beginning to take on a certain elegance, its plain tapering body standing on a shallow moulded foot and its hinged cover having a high dome with a moulded rim. Spouts were sometimes at right angles to the handle. Early Georgian coffee pots were generally cylindrical or polygonal, with matching domed lids. A graceful swan-neck spout replaced the previous tubular type. Rotund coffee pots were also made concurrently with this style. These were pear-shaped and were favoured by Huguenot silversmiths, while the straight-sided examples were usually preferred by English silversmiths, although this is only a generalisation. Decoration might be by cut-card work and covers were often fluted. Other coffee pots remained undecorated or perhaps engraved with a coat-of-arms. Paul de Lamerie designed a pear-shaped coffee pot in 1730 which was distinctive, being superbly chased with cupids and scrolls, the foot rim replaced by three intriguing feet formed as dolphins. The short spout was shaped as an eagle's head. This was typical of the much-favoured rococo decoration of that time.

Neo-classical coffee pots which were made during the last thirty years or so of the eighteenth century were generally based on the classical vase shape, standing upon a moulded, spreading foot, circular or square. The high covers with their urn-shaped finials were decorated to match or complement the feet and lower part of the body which would be commonly ornamented by convex spiral fluting. Other decoration included acanthus leaves, rams' heads, running floral scrolls, swags of foliage and ribbon bows. Decorative moulding was also widely used.

Nineteenth century designs included a melon shape with six or eight wide lobes, while during the 1830's and 1840's straight-sided coffee pots enjoyed a revival, circular, hexagonal and octagonal, their lids crowned by flowers and naturalistic ornament. Others were later made in a revived rococo or neo-classical style.

Early coffee pots generally have their hallmarks punched in a line near the top of the body below the rim. Later examples, from about 1760 are usually punched on the base.

Dish Rings

Dish rings often puzzle collectors, since their purpose seems ambiguous. They were mostly made in Ireland and it is generally thought that they were used to prevent heat marks from disfiguring the surface of the table. They stand about three inches high by approximately eight inches in diameter, although these measurements vary. Among the earliest examples are those produced during the reign of Queen Anne, but English dish rings are well outnumbered by those from Ireland, and in Dublin they were made in numbers from about 1745 onwards and increasingly so after about 1760. In appearance they resemble a giant napkin ring, but with pierced sides, usually very beautiful.

Another name for the dish ring is the potato ring, one theory being that they were stood upon a plate to contain hot potatoes, but dish rings appears to have been their description at the Dublin Assay Office. The body of the ring was formed from a sheet of silver about twenty inches long. This was rolled into a cylinder and hammered into a spool shape on a wooden block. The ends were then soldered together. Dish rings made between approximately 1760 to 1780 were wonderful examples of the silversmith's craft. They were beautifully worked in low relief repoussé, typified by pierced designs of figures, birds, fruit, flowers and scrolls. The open-work panels, linked by ornamental motifs, often consisted of a vigorously worked scene, perhaps harvesters gathering fruit, shepherds and shepherdesses, cottages and animals. Sometimes these might be based on legends.

With advances in manufacturing technques, the exquisite hand work which had been so marvellously imaginative and inventive declined. The background ceased to be cut away by hand, and instead embossed and chased ornament was produced separately, generally by the fly-press, then applied to the rings over open-work trellis. By the last two decades of the eighteenth century designs were becoming increasingly more repetitive, with vertical pierced pales of consistent patterns, heightened by applied festoons and drapery, or similar ornament, perhaps also bright cut. Later examples eliminated the need to apply the classic decoration because this, too, was incorporated in the work performed by the fly-press

Dish rings were usually hallmarked on the outside of the lower rim. The town mark (Dublin) and the standard mark should be punched, but the date mark may be missing. Others may have just the maker's mark. Many bogus reproductions have been made, so the utmost caution is required when buying one of these charming, if redundant, pieces of table silver.

Dish Crosses

These more utilitarian objects first originated in about the 1730's and, although ingenious, cannot be described as beautiful like the charming Irish dish ring. The dish cross, however, fulfilled a similar purpose from the 1750's onwards. It prevented the hot dish from marking the surface of the table and, since it also incorporated a spirit lamp, it kept the food warm at the same time. It consisted of two pairs of arms, which stood upon four legs. The arms crossed centrally, like the letter 'x', and beneath this point was incorporated the spirit lamp. Affixed to each arm was a bracket to hold the dish clear of the flames, and the length of the arms could be altered to accommodate the dish.

Cheese Toasters

This useful little utensil was invented during the reign of George III for the inexpensive, but succulent delights of toasted cheese. Most homes soon possessed one, if not in silver, then in Sheffield plate.

The cheese toaster consisted of an oblong covered pan with dishes or pans into which would go toasted bread covered with thin slices of cheese (Lancashire cheese was much favoured). The toast was kept warm from beneath, where there was a hot-water compartment. The water was poured in through the handle which unscrewed, or through an opening in the side of the toaster which had a cap. A chain was fastened to the cover of the toaster which raised the cover while the toaster was on the fire, reflecting the heat and hastening the cheese to bubble and brown. The hot-water compartment might be in Sheffield plate and the pans in hallmarked silver.

During the first two decades or so of the nineteenth century, some cheese toasters became more sophisticated in design. Their sides and covers were fluted and they stood on four decorative feet. Oval examples were also made from about 1815 with gadrooned sides and cover and a 'D' shaped handle at each end. Few cheese toasters were made after about 1830.

Table Baskets

Silver table baskets can be put to so many uses that their description has varied over the years. The entries in the Wakelin Ledgers of the 1770's describes them as 'bread baskets', at other times they have been called fruit baskets or cake baskets. Whatever their description they have been in constant use since seventeenth century and earlier.

The piercing of early baskets was laborious, the handwork needing great precision, even though the resultant piercing was inevitably large. However, with advances in the metal-rolling mill, Georgian silversmiths were able to produce more delicate work and pierced baskets, oval, rectangular and circular, expanded into an important branch of the industry.

Baskets by Huguenot silversmiths have won wide acclaim, although many superlative examples were also produced by London silversmiths. Typical of those made during the first three decades of the eighteenth century was the oval basket, with its base flat-chased around a central area intended for the coat-of-arms of the owner. The pierced sides might be interspersed with reeded straps. The small handles at each end were neatly cabled. A swing handle replaced these during the thirties, and by the end of this decade a shaped and decoratively pierced 'skirt' was added to the base which meant that the bottom of the basket was concealed from view.

By the 1740's everted rims were so shaped as to allow as much as possible of the interior of the sides to be seen at a glance. Some baskets stood upon four decorative feet. The rims and outer borders carried through the main decorative theme of the intricate piercing, and were often curved or scalloped, perhaps

44.   *Silver wire-work basket, 1763.*

incorporating chased and applied work of rococo influence. Masks in high relief might also be incorporated in the form of faces, cherubs' heads, lions or sometimes flowers. The intricate piercing consisted of all-over patterns comprising scrolls, circles, crescents and diamonds.

Later baskets became even more elaborate. The panels were finely pierced with geometrical motifs including quatrefoils, diapers, crosses and circles, perhaps alternating with panels pierced with foliated scrolls. Sometimes many elaborately pierced panels might go into the making of a single basket. These were made individually, then soldered together to form the oval basket. Joins were skilfully concealed by decorative beading, a 'ribbon' of which was produced mechanically.

Thus silversmiths fully exploited the complex degree of piercing made possible by the new fly-presses, which could punch intricate patterns with increasing accuracy and speed. At the same time, however, there were disadvantages. Quality was suffering. By the last two decades of the eighteenth century these less expensive factory-produced baskets were becoming shallow and light. Their piercing, too, declined. It became far more repetitive, consisting of basic motifs and trellis work patterns.

Baskets produced from silver wire became fashionable in approximately 1760. The wire framework would be overlaid with decorative sprays of corn, floral and foliage ornament, grapes and vine leaves. Wirework was one of the cheapest ways of making this type of basket and the cost might be around £2.15.0d towards the end of the eighteenth century. Silver wire baskets were popular until about 1825.

CHAPTER 7

General Silver and Wine Silver

Candlesticks

The socket candlestick in silver was comparatively rare before the Restoration in 1660, after which date it was produced with increasing ambition in design and decoration. At this stage the stem was hammered up from a flat sheet of silver, and generally consisted of architecturally inspired vertical columns arranged around the main stem to form a square. These were made separately and joined by soldering. They were then decorated with chased patterns. The stem stood upon a beautifully ornamented square or octagonal foot. Other late seventeenth century candlesticks were similarly inspired, and were made in sets of two, four or six. Decoration included vertical fluting and reeding.

During the 1690's, stems were cast instead of hammered up from the flat. Some were cast in one piece, while others were cast in sections and soldered together. The cast baluster-shaped stem emerged from about 1680, modified from time to time, either undercorated or with gadrooning, perhaps with an octagonal or hexagonal stem and a steeply rising foot. By the 1730's rococo decorated candlesticks became objects of splendour, with the silversmith lavishing all manner of ornament upon them. The baluster shoulders might be encrusted with applied masks moulded in full relief, and the stem with birds, monsters, torches, fruit and foliate motifs, scrolls and shells. Less exuberant decoration which remained in fashion until the 1760's was based on superlative chasing including scrolls and floral patterns. Undecorated, plain baluster candlesticks were made alongside the decorated.

The baluster-shaped candlestick looked somewhat homely against the new arrivals of the neo-classical period. These elegant candlesticks possessed a dignity which it was hard to rival. The Corinthian column was one main source of inspiration, its base raised upon a square pedestal with wreaths, draperies or some other classically inspired decoration. The socket inside the column contained a loose nozzle. These candlesticks were usually cast until approximately 1770 when, in order to keep costs down, they were produced from thin sheets of silver, their parts stamped out, then soldered together. The first factory-produced candlesticks of this type were weighted with pitch, but as increasingly thinner silver was made, lead was used.

Other neo-classical designs included a slender four-sided pedestal which tapered gracefully towards the foot, and which had a Grecian urn as its candle socket. Embellishments varied but were always drawn from neo-classical

45.   *A pair of cast candlesticks by Joseph Barbut, 1719. (Asprey and Company)*

inspiration and included rams heads, festoons of flowers and drapery and other typical motifs. Fashion dictated as well that the circular stem-shaped candlestick of the 1780's be fluted and taper to a circular base. These designs remained popular until the nineteenth century and to this day are copied prolifically.

Ornament on Regency candlesticks might be based on Egyptian inspired ideas, but they also underwent a revived rococo influence, although this usually lacked the originality and vivacity of its eighteenth century counterpart, as did the Victorian copies which were to follow. Victorian forms of decoration ranged from naturalistic derived ornament to Gothic and Greco-Roman ideas.

The demand for candelabra stems and branches reached its zenith from approximately the 1760's, and the introduction of Sheffield plate and weighted bases meant that they could be grander than ever at a relatively low cost. Candlesticks ranged in height from a mere nine inches to opulent candelabra of over two feet. Sometimes silver candlesticks have branches of Sheffield plate, either made for them originally or at a later date. Sets of smaller silver candlesticks were also made to match Sheffield plate candelabra.

Chamber Candlesticks and Snuffers

Chamber candlesticks (chambersticks) were intended for easy carrying, with a well-balanced and wide base which served as a drip tray, and a handle or finger ring to one side. The large house had many chambersticks, since they played a vital role in the lighting system. Without a chamberstick to light one along corridors and upstairs, life could prove hazardous. By approximately the 1720's the chamberstick might incorporate a pair of snuffers, a slot to hold these being in the dish beneath the candle-socket at the centre of the dish or base. A cone-shape extinguisher was also general. The socket with a detachable nozzle and a broader rim to catch the candle grease became more common a few years later.

Until approximately the 1810's, chambersticks were made in pairs and sets of varying numbers. They followed the changes in styles dominant during the eighteenth and nineteenth century. During the neo-classical period, an urn-shaped candle-socket lent elegance to the chamberstick, and the dish was rectangular, sometimes with four ball feet. Ornament included gadrooning, reeding and beading. Those made during the Regency era might have a larger dish heavily adorned with naturalistic and shell ornament. Victorian chambersticks usually favoured the circular dish.

Snuffers

Queen Victoria was on the throne before the non-guttering candlestick was introduced. Until this time snuffers were vital to trim the tallow or wax wick for two reasons. When the tallow wick was extinguished badly it gave off an unpleasant aroma, and also in order to have a consistent light, the wick required constant trimming because the tallow or wax melted faster than the wick burned. Snuffers were therefore essential. They resembled a pair of scissors, having a box

47. *A rare pair of early eighteenth century chambersticks, c.1715. (Asprey and Company)*

soldered to one blade into which fell the charred pieces of wick (snuff), snipped off by the 'scissors'.

Many snuffers were quite plain, perhaps the box decorated by engraving or fluting. The box varied in shape, generally rectangular, although it might also be oval, lozenge or like a barrel. After about the 1750's three little feet were attached to the base of many snuffers, one positioned beneath each handle and the box.

The prosaic pair of snuffers also took on a more decorative appearance. Handles became ornate. A coiled spring, concealed by a boss, was incorporated at the pivoting joint to ensure that they would stay closed. Later snuffers had steel blades and box, with silver handles so that they were far less expensive. Separate

46. *Facing Page: A pair of Corinthian column candlesticks by Ebenezer Coker, London, 1760. (Asprey and Company)*

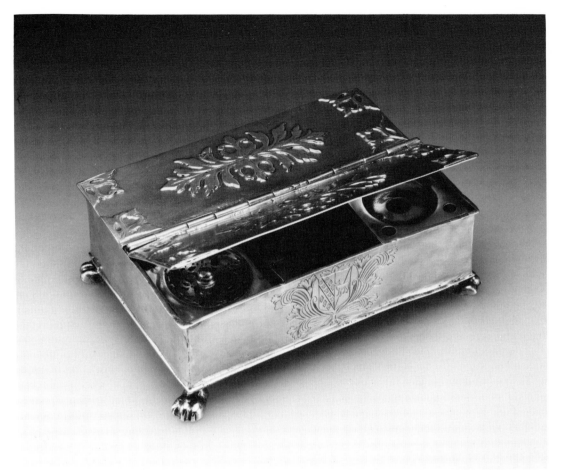

48. *A Charles II rectangular inkstand by John Ruslen, c.1677. (Asprey and Company)*

pieces were made by mass-produced methods then joined and decorated by the silversmith.

Dating from the rococo period the dish or tray which held the snuffers was often a thing of beauty in its own right. Until that time it had passed unnoticed, since the snuffers had generally been placed in a vertical socket on the dish. Now the dish began to reflect all the general trends in decoration and shapes, embracing a wide diversity of style. Those made during the nineteenth century were often elaborately embellished.

Tapersticks

Tapersticks, which looked like miniature candlesticks, in general stood approximately four to six inches in height. Their purpose was to house wax tapers which gave an instant flame, in the way that automatic lighting and friction matches did when they were invented. They were also known as tobacco candlesticks or tea candlesticks, and were put to various domestic uses.

Inkstands

Inkstands or standishes as they were referred to until approximately the early years of the nineteenth century, fell originally into two main designs. One design contained the inkpot, pounce or 'sand' box and wafer box in an oblong silver box with a hinged lid and perhaps a drawer below for quills; and a more familiar type had a tray on four feet, fitted with three sockets to hold the inkpot, wafer box and pounce box. (a wafer was a small adhesive disc, generally of flour mixed with gum and dyed red, which was used to seal letters). A delightful little hand bell for summoning a servant might replace the wafer box in some inkstands.

When mass-production methods lowered the cost of inkstands towards the end of the eighteenth century, flintglass began to replace the silver containers and costs were further lessened. Produced contemporaneously with these factory produced inkstands, however, were superlative hand-made examples. Designs popular during the late eighteenth century included a canoe-shaped tray with pierced sides, sometimes with a swing handle and a rectangular style, also pierced on the perimeter of the tray and often with complementing container sockets. Many shapes and designs followed during the nineteenth century and the production of inkstands was an important part of the Sheffield plate industry, in which their was a prolific output. Glass containers with silver mounts should be hallmarked, since although small, these were never exempt from hallmarking.

Pencils

Various types of propelling pencils and silver sheaths for pencils have entered the region labelled 'collectable' over recent years. Prices have gradually increased, therefore, but there are still bargains. Propelling pencils decorated or plain, have been made in reasonable quantity since the nineteenth century and early twentieth century. They are generally hallmarked, but not always, so make sure of this before paying the higher price which the sterling silver pencil commands.

The tightly fitting sheaths of silver which contain ordinary blacklead pencils, and which have pull-off covers are nearly always hallmarked, sometimes even including the small ring with which it might be hung from the person. These little sheaths can be attractive, nicely engraved, occasionally bright-cut, and nearly always containing their worn pencil. They make a satisfactory object to collect for beginners.

Scent Flasks and Bottles

Scent flasks of silver although rare are known of from Tudor times. Extant examples are usually chased and embossed with strapwork, or with additional fruit and foliate decoration. They mostly have pierced covers. Those shaped like pilgrim bottles have pendant chains.

Scent flasks for the general collector usually date from the nineteenth century, and the most charming of these are all-over decorated with engraved ornament, based on floral, foliate and scroll patterns. They are variously shaped. A heart was a popular form. Their covers or stoppers are often secured with a chain. Some silver flasks have a container for pills. Silver scent flasks should be hallmarked. Prominent among the nineteenth century makers of flasks was Sampson, Mordan and Company, a firm which made silver stoppers and mounts for perfume bottles. These outnumber flasks. They were commonly in coloured glass and with tightly fitting covers when intended for the handbag. Larger bottles were made for the dressing table. They were produced in a wide variety of shapes, often most attractive, and sometimes with the cover in a novelty form.

Frames

Silver frames, generally for photographs, became popular during the latter part of the nineteenth century, continuing into the twentieth century. The former were richly embossed and decorated, and were later joined by those in the style of *art nouveau* and *art deco.*

49. *Frame with overall floral and scroll decoration, made in 1905. (Sotheby's, Belgravia)*

50.   *Nineteenth century scent bottles. (Phillips)*

107

51.   *An owl scent flask with orange glass eyes by Charles and George Fox, London, 1846. (J. H. Bourdon-Smith Ltd.)*

52. *A fire engine scent flask which squirts scent rather than water by E. H. Stockwell, London, 1885. (J. H. Bourdon-Smith Ltd.)*

Wine Labels

Wine labels have long had a fascination for collectors, their incredible variety of design and names being the main reasons. They are also called bottle tickets and their original use, it is thought, was purely functional since they probably replaced the hand-written ticket which was generally attached to the pack thread on the cork of a bottle of wine. They originated during the second quarter of the eighteenth century when they were made by Sandilands Drinkwater.

Included among early wine label shapes was a narrow oblong, a crescent (much produced afterwards) and an escutcheon (shield). Many other designs joined these during the eighteenth and nineteenth centuries, used as they were to identify a wide diversity of brews, wines and cordials, as well as certain relishes. Decoration added to their charm as did their shapes. Wine labels might be formed like a vase, an elliptical disc, a vine leaf, scallop shell, anchor, goblet, cornucopia or Bacchanalian cherub. A fashionable kidney shape appeared after 1760, while the classically embellished goblet or star can generally be dated at around the last quarter of the eighteenth century. Decoration included reeding, bright-cutting, piercing and feather edging. Hand decorating was commonly replaced by die-stamping during the last decade or so, which in its turn was usually superseded by casting in the nineteenth century.

Wine labels were suspended from around the neck of the decanter (or bottle) by a chain, but others were made as plain 'collars' to fit over the neck, although these are seldom found earlier than about 1760. A third type, a plain rectangular, is hinged from a wire ring and was introduced at approximately the end of the eighteenth century and beginning of the nineteenth century. Vine leaf shaped labels date from the 1820's and those in the form of a cut-out initial appeared about ten years later. Single letters, upon small square labels, usually rather small, had been engraved earlier, but the new cut-out type of initial (the initial of the brew concerned) was cast separately, and was either chased or engraved.

The names on the labels present a great source of interest and amusement. 'Nig' was simply gin spelt backwards and dates from Victorian times when the master of the house did not wish his servants to know that he imbibed this 'working-class' alcohol, or the term was used as a disguise to stop the servants from drinking it. Wine bearing the label 'Vidonia' came from the Canary Islands; 'Mountain' from Malaga. 'Methuen' was another name for port.

Early wine labels are not generally hallmarked, perhaps bearing only the maker's mark or the lion passant. Those made after 1784 were subject to assay, however, and this was further clarified in the subsequent list of articles subject to hallmarking which was issued in 1790. Labels were also made for perfumed toilet waters like eau-de-Cologne. The demand for wine labels declined after 1860, when a Licensing Act ordered the labelling of bottles sold by retailers. Wine labels, because of their attraction, have continued to be made in comparatively small numbers throughout the years.

53. *Eighteenth century wine labels. (Phillips)*

Wine Funnels and Strainers

Wine funnels, functional and useful, are popular today as presents, even among those who do not profess to collect antique silver. The price, not surprisingly, often astonishes the unitiated. Those made during the first half of the eighteenth century are rare. They mostly date from the last three decades, possibly because at around this time it became increasingly more popular to decant wine into flint-glass decanters. One of the earliest recorded examples, c.1661, is in the Victoria and Albert Museum.

Sometimes they had an ornate rim, or might be shaped perhaps as an urn or in the ogee form. Some had a detachable strainer. Others incorporated a ribbed stem so that air bubbles might escape. A curved stem tip on certain examples (usually later) prevented aeration of the liquid while it was being decanted. Funnels used in general for pouring spirits into square decanters had straight spouts which tapered.

Strainers were much in use during the eighteenth century because of the imbibing of the much-favoured punch. They were described as 'orange strainers' in the Garrard Ledgers, but have also been referred to as lemon, punch and wine strainers. It is thought that when the smaller strainer was used, the orange or lemon juice which was vital for many punch recipes, would be strained into a smaller bowl and then poured into the punch. Larger strainers were made for use with the punch bowl. The piercing of strainers was often of a very high calibre, and in general they were of good quality. They had either two flat handles soldered to the rim, or a single handle.

54. Eighteenth century strainers made in London.

112

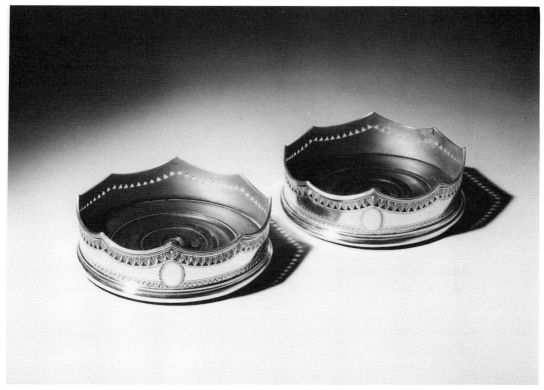

55. *Late eighteenth century wine coasters.*

Wine Coasters

Wine coasters were known variously as a 'wine slide', 'decanter stand', 'bottle stand' and 'bottle tray'. Their purpose was to protect the table surface as wine bottle or decanter were slid along the table. They came into fashion from approximately the 1760's and became increasingly popular with the growing use of the decanter. They might be sold singly or in sets of multiples of two. Certain early examples might have both base and rim of silver, but the majority had a boxwood base, covered beneath with green baize.

Coasters with pierced galleries were made from the late 1770's, the piercing automatically punched by the fly-press. Patterns included the popular idea of vertical pales with classical motifs. During the following decade undulating and escalloped rims enhanced the coaster, perhaps with a double row of horizontal piercing. By the last decade of the eighteenth century the top of the gallery was sometimes embossed or fluted and the lower part was pierced. This was later reversed. Coasters made during the Regency period might have a widely everted upper rim. Decoration included shell and scroll and, from around the second decade of the nineteenth century, ornament in general was distinctly heavy. From about 1790 the novelty type double coaster was made, perhaps in the form of a wagon or boat.

Tumbler Cups

These generally small vessels appeared from around 1650 and were made increasingly after this date. They were useful for the occupants of carriages when desirous of a little refreshment, since they retained, more or less, a vertical position. The silversmith achieved this by using a heavier silver on the rounded base than the sides, thus the tumbler cup righted itself before any liquid was spilled. Tumbler cups were made singly or in sets.

Stirrup Cups

The stirrup cup shaped like a fox's mask appeared in the 1760's This idea became popular with ensuing years and the head of the fox grew increasingly more realistic. There were also greyhounds' heads and occasionally a hare. Tapering, cylindrical bottles were produced from the early nineteenth century to fit a saddle bucket. Variously engraved mottoes included "Success to Foxhunting and the Joys of a Tally".

56.   Tumbler cup, London, 1727.

CHAPTER 8

Hallmarks

Collectors of silver should equip themselves with certain basic facts about the British hallmarking system. These are not difficult to assimilate, and are so intriguing historically that they generally inspire the desire for further reading on the subject.

For over six centuries hallmarks have acted as a safeguard for anybody who has bought gold or silver, and for this reason they may be described as probably the earliest form of consumer protection. They guarantee that an article has been tested at an Assay Office and that it conforms to one of the legal standards of fineness or purity. No article of silver or gold is made entirely of the respective precious metal because this is too soft. Silver and gold (and platinum) therefore need to be alloyed with base metals which immediately lower the value. Since it is not possible to assess what proportion of precious metal there is in an article by looking at it, chemical analysis is necessary. The Assay Offices in Britain are incorporated by Royal Charter or by statute, and all are independent of any trade organisation. When an article is submitted to one of them for testing, this is conducted by extremely accurate analyses, usually carried out on small samples removed from the object before it has been finally polished.

Nowadays there are four Assay Offices in England (London, Birmingham, Sheffield and Edinburgh), but in past times there were more. After 1 January 1975 these four Offices began to punch the same date letter on objects, but before this each used its own date letter. These change annually. If you want to date a piece, therefore, you must first discover where it was assayed, and then peruse the list of date letters for that Assay Office. You must, of course, know the mark of identification for each Assay Office (called the mark of origin), and collectors of antique silver will also need to learn the marks of origin of certain Assay Offices which have long since closed.

Foremost among the Assay Offices is that of London, whose links with antiquity reach back to the Middle Ages. The mark of origin for London is a leopard's head (the head bore a crown until 1822), which has more or less evolved into a mark of origin, since it was first introduced in 1300 following a statute by King Edward I as proof that the silver used in an object met the required standard as laid down by the law of the day. During the years between 1679 and 1720 – the time that the Britannia standard was enforced – it was replaced temporarily by the lion's head erased.

The crowned leopard's head was used by itself for some sixty-three years. Then another mark was added to it. A further ordinance decreed that "each Master Goldsmith should have a mark to himself . . . and after the assay has taken place, the supervisors shall put on the King's mark (the leopard's head), and then the goldsmith his mark". From this time on, therefore, there were two marks punched on silver objects, one of which was the maker's mark.

When King Edward I passed the statute directing the use of the leopard's head, it was also ordered that "in all the good towns of England, where there are goldsmiths . . . one shall go from each town for all the others to London to seek the sure touch". This meant that silver items made throughout England were also punched with the leopard's head. This was not always carried out in London. When other Assay Offices opened, silversmiths would take their wares to the office nearest to them.

The third mark, the date letter was introduced in 1478. A 20-letter cycle was used, without J and ending at U (also shaped like a V), and the letter was altered annually on 19 May (St. Dunstan's Day, see Chapter I). The type of lettering or the shield in which the letter was contained was changed with the new alphabet. Sometimes the shape might be altered during the year to indicate a change of assayer.

The fourth mark, the lion passant guardant appeared in 1544. It denoted that the metal was of sterling silver, that is 925 parts of pure silver per thousand.

These are the four basic marks still in use today, but collectors who take old silver seriously should also know about certain other marks. Britannia silver is the name for silver of a higher standard, first introduced between 1697 and 1720. During this period the standard of silver was raised from 925 fine to 958 fine. Demand for silver had risen to such heights that it exceeded the amount of bullion then obtainable. Some silversmiths were not above accepting parcels of silver which might contain melted-down coins or plate, which encouraged the practice of coin clipping and brought about a lack of confidence in the currency. Sometimes a coin might lose up to as much as one-fifth of its true weight. When the standard which was legally required for silver objects was raised, however, this then differed to that required for currency and the straightforward conversion was stopped.

The Britannia standard did not include Scottish or Irish silver, and during the years that it was used the hallmarks were: the Britannia mark (a seated figure of Britannia); a lion's head erased; the date letter; and the maker's mark, consisting of the first two letters of the maker's surname. After June 1720, the old sterling standard was restored and the hallmarks returned to those previously used, although silversmiths were allowed to produce objects of the Britannia standard if they wished. In 1738, a further statute decreed that goldsmiths should destroy their former marks and register new ones which were to be initials only, and of another type of lettering to preceeding marks.

A further mark of importance to collectors was introduced in 1784 and ceased after 1890. In 1784 an Act re-imposing a duty of sixpence on each ounce of silver was enforced. As an acknowledgement that the duty had been paid, the silver was punched with a shape of the sovereign's head. Specified pieces of small silver which were already exempt from hallmarking were not included in the re-imposed duty.

Birmingham Assay Office and Sheffield Assay Office

The Birmingham and Sheffield Assay Offices, although established only in the late eighteenth century, quickly grew to importance. Rapid advances in mechanism and the subsequent progress in mass-production which brought down costs, resulted in an overwhelming demand for silver wares. Silversmiths in Birmingham and Sheffield grew weary of taking their wares to the nearest Assay Offices to be marked – a trek to Chester for Birmingham silversmiths, and Chester or York for those of Sheffield, with London as an alternative. Matthew Boulton, a highly respected and influential Birmingham manufacturer of metal goods, decided that the time had come for an Assay Office in Birmingham. He quickly gained the support of other craftsmen and local influential gentry.

His attempts reached the ears of The Sheffield Cutlers' Company. In 1772 Matthew Boulton was the recipient of a letter from their clerk which requested that they should be included in his proposals, in order that the two towns might join together in petitioning Parliament. As a result of a Parliamentary Committee's Enquiry in 1773 and the petition, an Act for appointing Wardens and Assay Masters for assaying wrought plate in the towns of Birmingham and Sheffield was passed in 1773. At the same time the Act forbade the stamping of any letters upon any manufactured article of metal plated, or covered with, or looking like silver. A modification eleven years later permitted manufacturers of plated goods within 100 miles of Sheffield to strike their surnames or the name of their partnership with some device alongside, but they were not to bear any likeness to a hallmark, and were required to be registered at the Assay Office.

The place of origin mark for Birmingham was an anchor which was struck either vertically or horizontally, and that for Sheffield was a crown. The crown was replaced by a rose under the Statute of 1973. The Birmingham Assay Office initially used an alphabet of twenty-five date letters (omitting J) which was changed annually in July. The alphabet which began in 1798 employed twenty-six letters. The proceeding one, which began in 1824, reverted to twenty-five letters. That for the period beginning 1849 used twenty-six letters. From 1875 the alphabet used has consisted of twenty-five letters. Sheffield used a varied selection of date letters. By 1868 a twenty-five letter cycle was regulated. From 1780 to 1853 a combined punch of the crown and date letter was usual.

Other Provincial Assay Offices

In 1700 a statute set up Assay Offices in towns where there were mints which included York, Exeter, Bristol, Chester and Norwich. This determined such matters as the election of Wardens, the appointment of a skilled assayer and the keeping of a Diet Box. Some of the scrapings from each object submitted for assaying were to be placed in the Diet Box and tested annually by the Royal Mint to ensure that provincial assayers were maintaining the right degree of accuracy.

57. *Mark of origin for London*

58. *Mark of origin for Birmingham*

59. *Mark of origin for Sheffield prior to 1975*

60. *Mark of origin for Edinburgh*

61. *Mark of origin for Glasgow*

62. *Mark of origin for Dublin*

63. *Mark of origin for Exeter*

64. *Mark of origin for Chester*

65. *Mark of origin for Newcastle*

Bristol Assay Office

The mark of origin for Bristol was a ship issuing from a castle. An earlier mark is assumed to have been a BR in monogram. It is thought that the Bristol Assay Office was functioning between 1720 and 1740. Bristol area silversmiths then took their products to Exeter to be hallmarked. After approximately the mid-nineteenth century the wares from Bristol accounted for more than sixty per cent of pieces assayed at the Exeter Assay Office.

Chester Assay Office

Although moneyers were working at Chester from Saxon days, no reference to Chester appears in the usual Acts. In 1686–87, the goldsmiths of the town drew up a statement of intent, citing all legislation relevant to the standards of gold and silver from the year 1300. The Wardens' marks were to be the coat-of-arms and crest of the City of Chester on two individual punches, the crest being a sheathed sword, point uppermost, and belt attached, resting on an orle. The coat-of-arms of the City was a sword erect between three wheat sheaves. In 1700 a new Assay Office came into being and the town mark used was the new version of the city arms, three demi-lions passant and one-and-a-half wheat sheaves. It was in use until 1777, then the ancient arms of the city were re-instated, and used until the Assay Office closed in 1962.

Exeter Assay Office

The mark of origin for Exeter was the triple-towered castle, taken from the city's coat-of-arms. It was used in conjunction with a date letter alphabet of twenty-four letters (excluding J and U), changed each year on 7 August. The office closed in 1883.

Newcastle Assay Office

The mark of origin for Newcastle, taken from the city's coat-of-arms consisted of three towers. A variable series of date letters was used. The office closed in 1884.

Norwich Assay Office

Marks of origin for Norwich include: a castle over a lion; a separate crown and rose; a crowned rose. The office closed shortly after 1701.

York Assay Office

York was the second most important city in England during the Middle Ages. Goldsmiths had their own touch mark and a town mark in 1411. This was half a leopard's head with half a fleur-de-lys, conjoined in a circular punch. It was changed in 1701 to five lions passant on a cross. From 1778 this was enclosed in a shield. Nine years later an oval replaced the shield. The office was closed in 1858.

Scotland

Edinburgh Assay Office

Silver bearing Scottish marks can be dated as early as the middle of the fifteenth century. By 1681 the Goldsmiths of Edinburgh were using a variable date letter

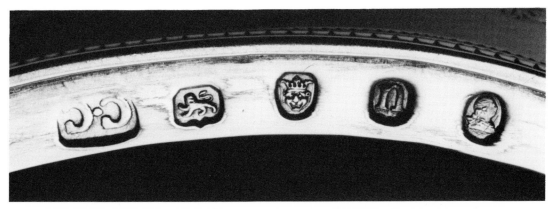

66. *These marks on a neo-classical mustard pot read, from left to right: CC (Charles Chesterman), lion passant or sterling lion, leopard's head crowned (mark of origin for London) 'n', date for 1788 and the sovereign's head which showed that duty had been paid. (The Colman Collection)*

and were no longer using the deacon's mark instituted in 1475, taking instead the mark of the Assay Master. In 1759 this was abandoned and a thistle replaced it. The town mark is a triple-towered castle.

Glasgow Assay Office

Although goldsmiths worked in Glasgow from the sixteenth century, no Glasgow silver earlier than around 1681 appears to have been documented with marks other than sometimes the maker's mark and burgh arms – a tree with a bird on the top, a hand bell suspended from the branches and across, or below, the trunk a salmon with a ring in its mouth. This is called the fish, tree and bell mark. A date letter was regularised in 1819. The office closed in 1964.

From approximately 1730 to around 1800, the letter S in a shaped punch which was varied, was also commonly used. It probably meant 'Sterling' or 'Standard Quality'. The marks for Glasgow, after an Act of 1819, which constituted the Glasgow Goldsmiths' Company a body corporate, were the date letter, the lion rampant (from the Royal Standard of Scotland) which was used as the standard mark, the town mark, maker's mark and sovereign's duty mark.

(Note: In Scotland the sovereign's head was struck on silver after 1784 – in common with England – to show that duty had been paid. However, there was not uncommonly a delay in the change of the head following the accession of a new monarch. The head of Queen Victoria was not stamped on Edinburgh silver until about four years after she had ascended the throne).

Edinburgh and Glasgow were both important Assay Offices. Other towns where silver was marked included Canongate (now a part of Edinburgh), Aberdeen, Arbroath, Dundee, Elgin, Greenock, Inverness, Montrose, Perth, Tain and Wick.

121

Irish Silver

A Royal Charter was granted by Charles I to Dublin Goldsmiths in 1637, yet goldsmiths had worked in Ireland far earlier. The Charter decreed that their silver was to bear the mark of the harp crowned – the King's Majesty's stamp and the standard of fineness – together with the mark of the maker. A varied date letter was used irregularly from 1638.

Approximately ten years after the old sterling standard was restored in England and the figure of Britannia was no longer in general use, the figure of Hibernia was added to Dublin silver. It represented a tax. At this time the Irish Parliament taxed certain items of silver to raise funds for agricultural improvements. Hibernia stamped on articles was proof that the tax had been paid. The head of the sovereign – the duty mark used in England – was stamped from 1807 to 1890, replacing that of Hibernia as a duty mark. However, Hibernia was still used and represented the town mark of Dublin.

The assaying of Dublin silver was inconsistent. Silver was sometimes left unmarked. Other pieces might bear the crowned harp, Hibernia and a maker's mark. This applies to the years during the reigns of George II and George III. The year letter was not used, so objects cannot be specifically dated by the marks. Until around 1850 the maker's mark usually consisted of the initials of the christian and surname, separate or monongrammed, and might be crowned or used in conjunction with an emblem until about 1760. During the nineteenth century the entire surname might be used.

Irish silversmiths not uncommonly ignored the law when it came to having their work assayed in Dublin. Seeking to avoid the payment of duty necessary from 1730, their wares might be marked inconsistently and sometimes with their own devices.

London

Year	Mark	Year	Mark	Year	Mark	Year	Mark	Year	Mark	Year	Mark	Year	Mark
1678	a	1686		1696		1705		1715		1724		1732	R
1679	b	1687		1697		1706		1716	A	1725	K	1733	S
1680	c	1688		1698		1707		1717	B	1726	L	1734	T
1681	d	1689	m	1699		1708		1718	C	1727	M	1735	V
1682	e	1690	n	1700		1709		1719	D	1728	N	1736	a
1683	f	1691	o	1701	ff	1710		1720	E	1729	O	1737	b
1684	g	1692	p	1702		1711		1721	F	1730	P	1738	C
1685	h	1693	q	1703	B	1712		1722	G	1731	Q	1739	d
		1694	r	1704		1713		1723	H			1739	d
		1695	s			1714							

122

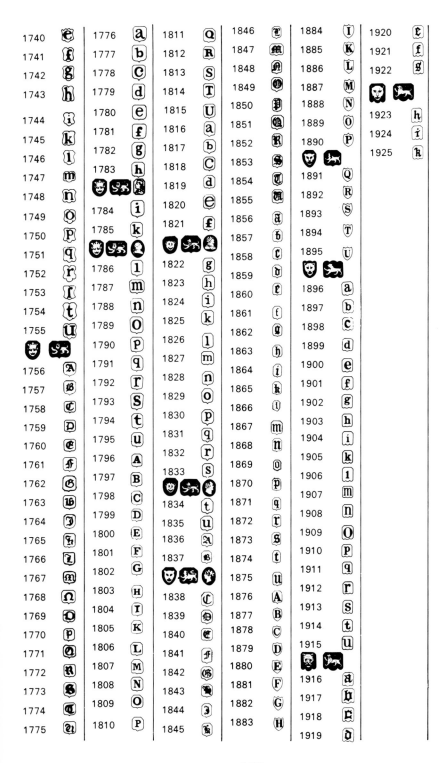

Birmingham

Year	Letter	Year	Letter	Year	Letter	Year	Letter	Year	Letter
1773	A	1801	d	1837	O	1873	Y	1908	i
1774	B	1802	e	1838	P	1874	Z	1909	k
1775	C	1803	f	1839	Q	1875	a	1910	l
1776	D	1804	g	1840	R	1876	b	1911	m
1777	E	1805	h	1841	S	1877	c	1912	n
1778	F	1806	i	1842	T	1878	d	1913	o
1779	G	1807	J	1843	U	1879	e	1914	p
1780	H	1808	k	1844	V	1880	f	1915	q
1781	I	1809	l	1845	W	1881	g	1916	r
1782	K	1810	m	1846	X	1882	h	1917	s
1783	L	1811	n	1847	Y	1883	i	1918	t
1784	M	1812	o	1848	Z	1884	k	1919	u
1785	N	1813	p	1849	A	1885	l	1920	v
1786	O	1814	q	1850	B	1886	m	1921	w
1787	P	1815	r	1851	C	1887	n	1922	x
1788	Q	1816	s	1852	D	1888	o	1923	y
1789	R	1817	t	1853	E	1889	p	1924	z
1790	S	1818	u	1854	F	1890	q	1925	A
1791	T	1819	v	1855	G	1891	r		
1792	U	1820	w	1856	H	1892	s		
1793	V	1821	x	1857	I	1893	t		
1794	W	1822	y	1858	J	1894	u		
1795	X	1823	z	1859	K	1895	v		
1796	Y	1824	A	1860	L	1896	w		
1797	Z	1825	B	1861	M	1897	x		
1798	a	1826	C	1862	N	1898	y		
1799	b	1827	D	1863	O	1899	z		
1800	c	1828	E	1864	P	1900	a		
		1829	F	1865	Q	1901	b		
		1830	G	1866	R	1902	c		
		1831	H	1867	S	1903	d		
		1832	J	1868	T	1904	e		
		1833	K	1869	U	1905	f		
		1834	L	1870	V	1906	g		
		1835	M	1871	W	1907	h		
		1836	N	1872	X				

Sheffield

Year	Mark	Year	Mark	Year	Mark	Year	Mark	Year	Mark	Year	Mark	Year	Mark
(lion / crown)		1793	o	1816	T	1838	S	1860	S	1882	P	1905	n
1773	E	1794	m	1817	X	1839	t	1861	S	1883	Q	1906	o
1774	F	1795	q	1818	I	(lion / crown / head)		1862	(symbols)	1884	R	1907	p
1775	H	1796	Z	1819	V	1840	u	1863	U	1885	R	1908	q
1776	R	1797	X	1820	Q	1841	V	1864	W	1886	S	1909	r
1777	h	1798	V	1821	Y	1842	X	1865	X	1887	U	1910	s
1778	S	1799	E	1822	Z	1843	Z	1866	Y	1888	V	1911	t
1779	A	1800	N	1823	U	1844	A	1867	Z	1889	W	1912	u
1780	Z	1801	H	1824	a	1845	B	(symbols)		1890	X	1913	v
1781	D	1802	M	1825	b	1846	C	1868	A	(crown / lion)		(crown / lion)	
1782	G	1803	F	1826	c	1847	D	1869	B	1891	Y	1914	w
1783	B	1804	G	1827	d	1848	E	1870	C	1892	Z	1915	x
(lion / crown / head)		1805	B	1828	e	1849	F	1871	D	1893	a	1916	y
1784	I	1806	A	1829	f	1850	G	1872	E	1894	b	1917	z
1785	V	1807	S	1830	g	1851	H	1873	F	1895	c	(crown / lion)	
(lion / crown / head)		1808	P	1831	h	1852	I	1874	G	1896	d	1918	a
1786	k	1809	K	1832	k	1853	K	1875	H	1897	e	1919	b
1787	C	1810	L	1833	l	1854	L	1876	J	1898	f	1920	c
1788	m	1811	C	(symbols)		1855	M	1877	K	1899	g	1921	d
1789	M	1812	D	1834	m	1856	N	1878	L	1900	h	1922	e
1790	L	1813	R	1835	p	1857	O	1879	M	1901	i	1923	f
1791	P	1814	W	1836	q	1858	P	1880	N	1902	k	1924	g
1792	u	1815	O	1837	r	1859	R	1881	O	1903	l	1925	h
										1904	m		

Edinburgh

Year	Mark	Year	Mark	Year	Mark	Year	Mark	Year	Mark	Year	Mark	Year	Mark
(castle)		1715	L	1727	X	1739	K	1751	W	1761	G	1773	T
		1716	M	1728	Y	1740	L	1752	X	1762	H	1774	U
1705	A	1717	N	1729	Z	1741	M	1753	Y	1763	I	1775	V
1706	B	1718	O	1730	A	1742	N	1754	Z	1764	K	1776	X
1707	C	1719	P	1731	B	1743	O	1755	A	1765	L	1777	W
1708	D	1720	Q	1732	C	1744	P	1756	B	1766	M	1778	Z
1709	E	1721	R	1733	D	1745	Q	1757	C	1767	N	1779	YA
1710	F	1722	S	1734	E	1746	R	1758	D	1768	O	1780	A
1711	G	1723	T	1735	F	1747	S	(castle / thistle)		1769	P	1781	B
1712	H	1724	U	1736	G	1748	T	1759	E	1770	Q	1782	C
1713	I	1725	V	1737	H	1749	U	1760	F	1771	R	1783	D
1714	K	1726	W	1738	I	1750	V			1772	S		

Edinburgh

Year	Mark	Year	Mark	Year	Mark	Year	Mark	Year	Mark	Year	Mark	Year	Mark
(castle) (thistle) (head)		1803	X	1823	r	1843	M	1864	H	1885	d	1905	Z
1784	E	1804	Y	1824	S	1844	N	1865	I	1886	e	1906	A
1785	F	1805	Z	1825	t	1845	O	1866	K	1887	f	1907	B
(castle) (thistle) (head)		1806	a	1826	u	1846	P	1867	L	1888	g	1908	C
1786	G	1807	b	1827	v	1847	Q	1868	M	1889	h	1909	D
1787	G	1808	c	1828	w	1848	R	1869	N	1890	i	1910	E
1788	H	1809	d	1829	x	1849	S	1870	O	(castle) (thistle)		1911	F
1789	IJ	1810	e	1830	y	1850	T	1871	P	1891	k	1912	G
1790	K	1811	f	1831	z	1851	H	1872	Q	1892	l	1913	H
1791	L	1812	g	1832	A	1852	B	1873	R	1893	m	1914	I
1792	M	1813	h	1833	S	1853	W	1874	S	1894	n	1915	K
1793	N	1814	i	1834	C	1854	X	1875	T	1895	o	1916	L
1794	O	1815	j	1835	D	1855	B	1876	U	1896	p	1917	M
1795	P	1816	k	1836	E	1856	Z	1877	V	1897	q	1918	N
1796	Q	1817	l	1837	f	1857	A	1878	W	1898	r	1919	O
1797	R	1818	m	1838	G	1858	B	1879	X	1899	s	1920	P
1798	S	1819	n	1839	H	1859	C	1880	Y	1900	t	1921	Q
1799	T	(castle) (thistle) (head)		1840	J	1860	D	1881	Z	1901	u	1922	R
1800	U	1820	o	(castle) (thistle) (head) 1861	E	1862	F	1882	a	1902	w	1923	S
1801	V	1821	p	1841	K	1862	F	1883	b	1903	r	1924	T
1802	W	1822	q	1842	L	1863	G	1884	c	1904	y	1925	U

67. *The above assay marks are reproduced by courtesy of the Joint Committee of the Assay Offices of Great Britain.*

CHAPTER 9

Pitfalls for Collectors

Generally speaking, the collector can rely upon hallmarks to give a correct indication of purity and date. However, as mentioned earlier, all collectors should avail themselves of a knowledge of fashion, styles, decoration and techniques. This knowledge combined with that of the British hallmarking system will serve them in good stead against possible forgeries. Happily, these are rare, but undoubtedly they do exist.

In the main they come into the category of transferred hallmarks, an easy procedure for the dishonest craftsman. He simply removes a perfect set of hallmarks from, perhaps, a worn or broken earlier object and incorporates them into a more recent or less valuable object, which is immediately raised in value. If in doubt, breathe hard on the hallmark (or anywhere else where you think there has been a repair or unscrupulous work) and the outlines of the let-in silver or joins will often become apparent.

Vessels are sometimes altered because their conversion will command a higher price or be more in demand with current fashion. A tankard, for example, can be converted into a hot-water jug; mugs transformed into jugs;and in other cases, early spoons with worn bowls (with trifid ends) can become valuable three-pronged forks. Eighteenth century teaspoons will sell for a higher price if they are converted into mote skimmers. Apostle spoons can be produced by hammering into the correct shape the bowls of ordinary spoons and finished off with an apostle finial. The silver lid of a small glass jar can become a delectable eighteenth century button. Vinaigrettes with broken pierced inner lids can be given an instant 'face life' by the insertion of a pierced lid from a similar, defunct vinaigrette. After a while the collector develops a sort of detecting antennae which give warning signals when something seems suspicious. Before this degree of atunement is reached, however, remember to check with care all hallmarks. A repaired coffee jug, for instance, with a lid that is not the original is hardly likely to have the same hallmarks on the body as those on the lid.

The collector of small items should familiarise himself with the list of items exempt from hallmarking. The Plate Offences Act, 1738 (An Act for the Better Preventing of Frauds and Abuses in Gold and Silver Wares) exempted many smaller articles from assay. These included: thimbles, stone-set jewellery, book clasps and "very small nutmeg graters, rims of snuff boxes whereof Top or Bottoms are made of Shell or Stone, Sliding Pencils, Toothpick Cases, Tweezer Cases, Pencil Cases, any Filigree Work, and Mounts, Screws or Stoppers to Stone or Glass Bottles or Phials, any small or slight Ornament put to Amber or other

Eggs or Urns, or any Gold or silver so richly engraved, carved or chased or set with Jewels or other Stones, as not to admit an Assay to be taken of, or a Mark to be struck thereon, without damaging, prejudicing, defacing the same, or such other things as by reason of the smallness or thinness thereof are not capable of receiving the Marks, herein before mentioned or any of them, not weighing Tenpenny Weights of Gold or Silver each".

The Duty Act of 1784 was further passed with these exemptions, but its ambiguous wording necessitated a more precise list in 1790. At this time more exemptions were added to the list. These included "Tippings, Swages or Mounts or any of them not weighing tenpenny weights of silver each".

Important, indeed, is it to note the objects which, at this time were *excluded* from exemption on the list. Such items weighing under fivepenny weights included the following: necks, collars and tops of casters, cruets or glasses, appertaining to any sort of stands or frames, bottle tickets, shoe clasps, patch boxes, salt spoons, salt shovels, salt ladles, tea spoons, tea strainers, caddy ladles, and pieces to garnish cabinets or knife cases or tea chests, bridles or stands or frames.

It can be said in general, therefore, that from 1738 to 1784 (effectively, also, until 1790), objects which weighed up to tenpenny weights or less may be found unmarked, after which certain wares weighing less than five penny weights are exempt. Remember, though, that they may still be hallmarked, should the manufacturer desire it. Before 1738, the marking of small objects was variable. While some were unmarked, there are others which are marked.

Apart from small objects, there are in circulation larger pieces with no marks, and this can be perplexing. There sometimes appears to be no reason for this, so that if an item really pleases the collector, and style and decoration seem right for the assessed date, he can always satisfy himself by seeking more valid proof of the silver content in the form of chemical analysis. He should remember, though, that unmarked pieces may command a less high price, than marked counterparts. And when the time comes to sell the object, this will be taken into consideration by the purchaser.

Earlier eighteenth century forks and spoons usually had their marks punched on the lower, narrow part of the stem. This often resulted in a flattening of the stem which had to be hammered up again into shape after hallmarking. Because of this the marks were frequently distorted – although they are still decipherable with the aid of a magnifying glass. This led, in general, to the change to top marking of the stems of forks and spoons by about 1782. As far as spoon makers are concerned, their marks would have been entered in the Small Workers' Register 1739–1758, but sadly this volume, together with the Large Workers' Register 1758–1773, were submitted in evidence to the 1773 House of Commons committee and never returned. Makers marks for these two periods are, therefore, not easy to identify unless there is an additional form of evidence.

Spoons by Thomas Chawner are an exception. There is proof that Thomas Chawner, who was made free in 1762, was in partnership with William Chawner in Red Lion Street, Clerkenwell, and since they are the only known spoonmakers with the right initials, the mark $W^T_C C$ is generally assumed to be theirs. Among the spoonmakers were: Daniel Smith and Robert Sharp (1763–96); John Crouch and Thomas Hannam (1766–93); George Heming and William Chawner (1773–81); Charles Aldridge and Henry Green (1713–82); and John Wakelin and William Taylor (1786–96). Makers' marks can be difficult to identify. Of great assistance can be *English Goldsmiths and their Marks* by Charles James Jackson, which is usually obtainable at good reference libraries.

Fakes and forgeries recorded by the Goldsmiths' Company (Goldsmiths' Hall, Foster Lane, London EC2) who mount exhibitions of a high calibre periodically, to which members of the public are admitted, have included some remarkable examples. Among these is a standing cup and cover in Sheffield plate, c.1770 (Sheffield City Museum). The marker's mark is HT in gothic script for Tudor and Leader of Sheffield. The makers have struck a form of their mark four times in a row beneath the rim so that the piece would appear to have been marked as for sterling silver. This sort of practice had to cease with the Statute of 1772–3 which imposed "a penalty of £100 against silversmiths and dealers who should strike any letter on metal, plated or covered with silver". It was not until 1784 that Sheffield plate manufacturers were again allowed to use marks. British plate, which evolved from Sheffield plate, but which had a silver-coloured base metal beneath the sterling silver instead of copper, was often marked with devices very closely resembling hallmarks.

Likewise, electro-plated items have quite commonly been garnished with the most delectable marks, looking for all the world as though they were the same as those appearing on contemporary pieces of sterling silver. The Victoria and Albert Museum have an electro-plated teapot of 1852, maker's mark, E & Co. crowned and E, M, & Co. all in separate punches for Elkington, Mason & Co. It is in the Régence style, chased with vertical bands of strapwork and the museum paid £3 for it in 1854. Elkington had begun making and marking electro-plated wares from 1840 (see Chapter II), and in 1841 introduced their own date letter system, which began with a figure I in a lozenge. The following year, Josiah Mason was brought in as a partner and additional marks, E, M, & Co in separate shields appeared. In 1849 the dating system was changed to letters of the alphabet, still in a lozenge, starting at K. The teapot is marked N and was thus made in 1852.

Apart from Sheffield plate and electro-plate marked with simulated hallmarks, there is a further type to remember. Pewterers quite commonly used marks on their wares which at a quick glance looked very much like hallmarks. The Victoria and Albert Museum has a jug of 1826 with pseudo marks of a dagger, leopard's head and cockerel. It is a barrel-banded jug with scroll handle and plain lip, engraved on the body with a monogram.

Items of dubious silver in the possession of The Goldsmiths' Company include a coffee pot altered from an Elizabethan communion cup; a tankard with fake marks T for 1774, leopard's head crowned, lion passant guardant, maker's mark, HB for Hester Bateman (an example of fake marks by Lyon and Twinam); a standing salt and cover, O for 1889, leopard's head, lion passant, sovereign's head, maker's mark, FE for Elkington and Company, which is an electrotype of the Mostyn salt of 1581 in the Victoria and Albert Museum, but the Assay Office did not notice and failed to obliterate the original Elizabethan hallmarks.

During the nineteenth century, London hallmarks were made in sizes varying in height from 1/4 in to 1/16 in. The smaller of these were placed in regular alignment, their punches contained in a frame, in order that they could be stamped quickly at one go. Certain pieces, made in the styles of earlier periods as legitimate reproductions, but not bearing the hallmarks of those periods, are therefore quickly recognisable.

Britannia silver is always respected and commands high prices. Because of this it is another potential field for the faker. Britannia silver is made today and will bear the Britannia mark. When this appears on pieces of a traditional design, a mechanical buffer may be used to all but obliterate the other marks, but leaving a 'worn' Britannia as bogus proof that the object is of early Britannia silver, worthy of the high price being asked for it.

There were always the dishonest silversmiths who managed to avoid paying duty. The ploys of the 'duty dodgers' mirrored largely their own inventiveness, but included the use of smaller marks, punched legitimately upon objects which they had sent for assay, then removed and inserted into a heavier piece.

CHAPTER 10

Sheffield Plate

Sheffield plate was to the eighteenth century what electro-plate became to the nineteenth and twentieth centuries. It enabled those, unable to afford the luxury of silver, to partake in the beauty and prestige of the appearance of this precious metal.

The diversity and range of objects which could be made in Sheffield plate was vast, and these, generally speaking, were of a good quality. Thomas Boulsover (1704–88) was the man who discovered this method of plating. In approximately 1742 he found that a sheet of silver could be fused by heat on to a thicker piece of copper. The fused metals were rolled from the ingot into a thin sheet of copper coated with a layer of silver. Thus, as far as appearances were concerned, the top side of the sheet looked like sterling silver. Boulsover confined his discovery mostly to the making of small objects. He took a partner (Joseph Wilson) and borrowed £170 to start a factory at Baker Hill, Sheffield, where he produced silver-plated buttons and buckles. He sold the buttons at a guinea a dozen -- the silver would have cost him about three shillings.

In addition to buttons and buckles, Boulsover later made small circular and oval boxes with pull-off lids and bases embossed in relief. However, Boulsover found it difficult to extend his range of products because he could not overcome one very important technical disadvantage. The red copper was apparent when the plated metal was sheared, and he could not find a way to conceal it. But a former apprentice of Boulsover's did find a way. This was Joseph Hancock, who quickly established himself as Boulsover's first truly serious competitor. He also had the foresight to instal horse power which meant that his pressure roller could reduce thicker ingots than formerly possible into larger sheets of plated silver. This immediately enabled him to produce objects of a wide variety of sizes.

Joseph Hancock entered the plating trade approximately nine years after Boulsover had first invented Sheffield plate (not known as Sheffield plate until around 1770), and began to produce a miscellaneous range of domestic tableware, emulating designs and styles produced by silversmiths. In 1762 Hancock acquired Thomas Boulsover's business.

Although the basic process of fusing silver and copper by heat was the same throughout the history of Sheffield plate, the range of wares was greatly extended when it was possible to silver both surfaces of the sheet of copper. Until this time hollow-wares like coffee pots and teapots were produced from single-plated copper and tinned inside, and this method continued for certain lidded hollow-ware after it became possible to silver both sides of the copper in the 1760's because it was far less expensive and also practicable. Teapots and other similar vessels could be re-tinned inside when necessary.

Despite the fact that Sheffield plate was a Sheffield discovery, it did not long remain solely worked there. Matthew Boulton, together with John Fothergill as his partner, established plating works at Soho, Birmingham, in 1762. He soon obtained a monopoly on its manufacture in Birmingham, establishing a reputation for quality work and becoming the largest manufacturer of Sheffield plate. The demand for Sheffield plate grew steadily. In 1784 a tax of sixpence an ounce was re-imposed on sterling silver (see Chapter 8), and because of this Sheffield plate became increasingly popular since the price of it was now approximately one-third of that for silver.

Although more effort and skill was required for producing Sheffield plated articles of fashion than was required for sterling silver (because of the nature of Sheffield plate which is discussed later), this was achieved by the determined Sheffield platers who produced fine-quality work. By the end of the eighteenth century, the number of Sheffield platers in Birmingham had risen to almost 100, and by the 1830's Birmingham seems to have taken over almost completely since there were then around ten silver platers working in Sheffield as against forty-seven in Birmingham.

Originally Sheffield plate was rolled and plated in the same factory that produced the wares. However, when plating grew into a specialised trade (the silvered plate was made in three standard qualities), the sheets of plated silver were sold to the makers of the wares. The men who hand-raised Sheffield plate were called braziers. They were competent craftsmen, working in the same ways as the silversmith, shaping hollow-wares from the flat plate with only basic tools – a steel stake for the shaping of the wares, upon which they worked with a wooden mallet as they hammered them into shape, proceeded by burnishing and decorating. Cylindrical hollow-wares were formed by folding the plate and joining at the seam, either dove-tail or but joints. The shape was perfected by hand hammering. The circular base was then soldered into place. Decorating followed, but before this the ware was beautifully polished by burnishing which also helped to conceal the joins, although these may often be discovered by examination with a magnifying glass. The finished surface although bright was never harsh, and today its mellow appearance much delights collectors.

An idiosyncrasy of Sheffield plate is the reddish tinge often discernible where the silver has worn thin through constant use. This can be attributed to fair wear and tear, but it would hardly have found favour with the Sheffield platers who liked their wares to emulate in every way that of their sterling silver counterparts. They disliked any tell-tale signs of copper. In particular they were conscious of the copper which was revealed along the edges where the Sheffield plate had been sheared. They overcame this finally by using a plated copper wire to conceal such edges. Sterling silver might also be used (c.1780–1830) on the more expensive wares, often decorated by hand chasing. The edges of Matthew Boulton's wares which used this method were marked with the words Silver Borders. Sheffield firms might use the wording Silver Edged. Sterling silver was later used for shields and mounts since it was impossible to engrave Sheffield plate as the copper would be revealed. In 1810 a method for rubbing-in silver shields was perfected, but before this they were soldered into position. When engraving on Sheffield plate was necessary, it was carried out on a very thick layer of silver.

The silver-lapped edge, in use from about the last twenty-five years of the eighteenth century to a few years over the first decade of the nineteenth, involved a U-shaped wire of sterling silver. It was made from a slender ribbon of wafer-thin silver which, when put through a hole in a draw-plate became a fine-bore tube. Its seams were then opened, resulting in a U-shape which was fitted over the edge of the Sheffield plate and soldered to the surface of both edges.

A patent was taken out in 1830 by Samuel Roberts for a plating process which finally concealed the colour of copper. It incorporated a layer of German silver (nickel silver) between the sterling silver and the copper. This meant that when the thin layer of sterling silver originally fused to the copper began to wear thin, revealing what lay beneath it, the German silver would show instead of the copper. German silver contained no silver. It was first made at Hildburghausen in Saxe-Meinengen and was an alloy of copper, zinc and nickel. Costs were also reduced by the use of German silver because less sterling silver was needed.

This method was superseded after about six years when further technical progress with German silver made this more malleable, and the use of copper was eliminated to be replaced entirely by German silver. The term British plate was used when advertising goods which were made from plate consisting of fused sterling silver and a silver-coloured nickel alloy. It could not truly be described as Sheffield plate. The lessening in costs, without the disadvantages of Sheffield plate, ensured it of considerble popularity until the introduction of electro-plate only a few years later, which quickly eclipsed it.

Methods of making objects in Sheffield plate followed tried and tested processes as well as new ones. The beginning of the 1770's saw the shaping of lids and spouts by the drop hammer (patented in 1769 by Richard Ford). The Sheffield plate would be placed on a striking block which had a die sunk with a model of the selected shape, then the hammer, the face of which was raised with the same face as the sunken die, was worked from above between two vertical rods and when it struck the block, the metal was shaped as the die. When technical progress produced harder steel, the object formed by the drop hammer became more precise in definition because the tools did not blunt so quickly. Later, after about the first fifteen years or so of the nineteenth century, entire units could be shaped like this.

In about 1820, hollow-ware was produced by lathe-spinning, replacing earlier hand raising, used when the number of objects required made it uneconomical to cut dies. In particular, large articles made during the 1820's and 1830's might be lathe-spun. Collectors may be able to discern for themselves when a piece was produced by lathe-spinning. If they examine the interior, faint circles can sometimes be seen where the piece was spun.

The decoration of Sheffield plate, as far as possible, echoed that used on contemporaneous sterling silver pieces. Eventually, decorative patterns were produced by the Sheffield plate factories of Sheffield and Birmingham, but before this the designs of the well-established London silversmiths were emulated and hand-craftsmen were used. Yet, since by its very composition, Sheffield plate presented difficulties not encountered by the silversmith, for example cracking which might lead to flaking and so reveal the copper, Sheffield plate craftsmen concentrated in general on line and proportion rather than too many intricacies of ornament.

Piercing, for example, much beloved on certain pieces of sterling silver, was impossible to execute on earlier Sheffield plate since cutting by the fret-saw could not be executed without revealing the copper beneath the silver. Pierced decoration on Sheffield plate, therefore, dates from the late 1760's when hand-operated fly-presses had steel tools with hardened tips which were designed to take a layer of silver from the face of the Sheffield plate, so that this extended beyond the sheared edge. The silver was then folded over to conceal the red of the copper. In the beginning each motif of the piercing was pressed separately, but by the middle of the last decade of the eighteenth century, the piercings were pressed in numbers. After the first two decades or so of the eighteenth century steam-operated presses came into use.

Embossing was vital if Sheffield platers were to truly rival the decorative effects achieved by the silversmith. However, this was not possible unless the copper was fused with a thicker than usual layer of silver – which was done – since the Sheffield plate might flake when the silver was stretched. Embossing was extremely fashionable until the last two decades of the eighteenth century and again from about 1820. It embellished a variety of domestic wares including jugs, bowls and tea services.

In 1822, William Mitchell, a silversmith of Glasgow, patented a press which simulated hand-chasing on flatware. In a single operation this could impress flowers, scrolls or diverse motifs on the plate. Flat chasing had embellished Sheffield plate from the 1780's including teapots, coffee pots, sugar basins, tea canisters, casters, salt cellars and mustard pots, commonly with piercing. Fluting and reeding were also general throughout the history of Sheffield plate, the parallel channels being either straight or in a slanting, spiral form. The rounded convex reeding, sometimes described as full-fluting, was fashionable during the last decade of the eighteenth century.

Engraving and bright-cutting presented further difficulties for the Sheffield plate craftsmen, since once again the copper was revealed by the graver. Bright cutting could not be ignored, however, since it appeared on so many sterling silver wares during the last decade of the eighteenth century. To compete, Sheffield plate manufacturers first bright-cut bands of sterling silver which were soldered

68. *Facing Page: Pair of Sheffield plate candlesticks by Boulton & Fothergill, c.1765. (Birmingham Assay Office)*
69. *Maker's marks: crown struck twice, B. & F.*

135

onto Sheffield plate. The band was generally about one inch wide. Bright-cutting on the actual Sheffield plate required a deeper layer of silver than was generally used, and this was another method which was employed.

Gilding was used for the interiors of certain vessels which did not have glass linings. It prevented corrosion or staining. Gilding was therefore used in salt cellars, mustard pots, cream jugs, punch bowls and various other appropriate items. Other hollow-wares were tinned inside, as already mentioned, a practice which continued into the 1820's. Trays and some pieces of flatware were also tinned, and the general effect was not unpleasing because the tinned surface was well polished at the factory.

Although Sheffield plate was used for an enormous diversity of objects, there are those for which it was particularly renowned. Among these was the candlestick. Candlestick making was considered one of the most important branches of the industry. Die-stamping was the technique employed. It kept down the costs and made this side of the business lucrative.

The production of inkstands was another important section of the Sheffield plate industry. The designs of these could be numbered in hundreds. Sheffield plate inkstands first appeared during the 1760's and were generally formed as a rectangular tray with a plain rim, four low scroll feet and dished channels for quill pens and penknife, with a raised platform for three flint-glass containers which had Sheffield plate tops. The term inkstand was used by Matthew Boulton in approximately 1770, to differentiate from the standish. Subsequently they followed, or were adapted from designs in sterling silver.

Among the 1,000 or so designs for inkstands were the inexpensive ones composed from plated wire of various sections. Plated wire was another branch of the Sheffield plate industry. It dated from the late 1760's. Fine strips of silver were fused onto copper rods. The plated rod was then repeatedly drawn through an instrument pierced with holes, starting at about an inch in diameter and decreasing down to the specific diameter required. The wire was used a great deal for numerous articles including fruit and cake baskets, sugar baskets and sugar vases.

Salt cellars were made in large numbers after about 1760, when open-work patterns lined with Bristol blue glass were popular. The salt cellars were usually oval at this stage, about one inch in depth, standing upon four small legs with ball and claw feet. Wavy rims in Sheffield plate were made from the mid 1770's. Salt cellars were produced in pairs and made in three qualities, tinned inside, plated inside with silver edges, or gilt inside with silver edges. (The first two were sold with blue glass liners). Neo-classical shapes followed. Melon shapes, eight lobed, alternating wide and narrow, were produced during the 1830's, as were rococo shell patterns. They continued to be produced in electro-plate.

70. Facing Page: Pierced sugar basket with swing, beaded handle. Sheffield plate. (Victoria and Albert Museum)

137

Identifying Sheffield plate by marks is seldom straightforward. Certain early pieces have distinguishing marks. However, it became illegal to mark Sheffield plate between 1773 and 1784 because of the resemblance of these marks with sterling silver hallmarks. After this date Sheffield plate manufacturers were allowed to use an emblem and the maker's name, although it was stipulated that such marks were not to be similar to hallmarks. This stipulation was ignored by some manufacturers who returned to the use of marks which might be confused with hallmarks. Other manufacturers did not bother to use a mark, despite the fact that fines were imposed for the lack of these.

After 1765, and increasingly following the turn of the nineteenth century, a crown was popularly used to accompany other marks. Joseph Hancock's mark c.1755 is recorded. His initials are punched similarly to those of contemporary London silversmiths. There does not appear to be a recorded mark for Thomas Boulsover. Other early initials include NS for Nathaniel Smith (1756); TL for Thomas Law, also Tho. Law in full (1758); TL for Tudor and Leader (1760); B & F for Boulton and Fothergill (1764); J S R for Jacob and Samuel Roberts (1765); IW for John Winter and Company (1765); M.Co for Richard Morton (1765); IR for J. Rowbotham and Company (1768); A E Co for Ashforth, Ellis and Company (1770); and J. L. PLATED for J. Littlewood (1772).

In addition to the crown which was used to denote quality and which was prohibited after 1896, other emblems used included the bell, open hand, the crossed arrows, the pineapple and the crossed keys. These should be remembered in particular since they have also been used on electro-plated articles. The bell was favoured, among others, by Roberts, Cadman and Company from c.1785; Roberts, Smith and Company from c.1828; and Smith, Sissons and Company from c.1848. The open hand by those including N. Smith and Company from c.1784; Smith, Tate and Nicholson and Hoult from c.1810; J. Watson and Son from c.1830; and Padley, Parkin and Company from c.1840. Other emblems were a ram's head, a bishop's mitre, a ship in full sail, a pipe, weighing scales, a unicorn, a fish, spoon and an umbrella, to name but a few. (See also Registration Marks in Chapter II).

Because of the vagaries of Sheffield plate marks, it is wise for collectors to have the receipts of expensive Sheffield plate fully worded to the effect that the piece was made prior to 1835. Towards the end of the nineteenth century and later, there was in circulation a type of plate which simulated old Sheffield plate, except that, although it had a copper foundation, the silver was electro-plated. Wares made by this method were often described as Sheffield plate when sold. In 1911, the Sheffield Cutlers' Company took action and obtained an injunction that the term 'Sheffield plate' should not be used for any pieces other than those made by the original method of fusing the silver and copper.

Despite the lack of reliable marks, there are other ways of ascertaining Sheffield plate. Foremost among these is the colour of the plate. By natural light this should be of a soft hue with a slightly bluish glow, very different to the hard colour of electro-plate. The lack of seams is a danger signal and can indicate that the piece was electro-plated. This may even apply if the shape of the piece is truly

71.   *Sheffield plate tea caddy c.1780. (Victoria and Albert Museum)*

right for the eighteenth century, since our Victorian forebears were accustomed to having their shabby articles re-plated by the new method of electro-plating. Pay attention to hinges. They should show the wear to be related to their age. Those on later imitations will be proportionately less worn.

Although Sheffield-plated wares were in the main of good quality, there was also an abundance of badly-plated wares which were imported from France and which had a ready market since they were so cheap. These were grossly inferior to Sheffield and Birmingham products. In appearance they appear what they are, lightweight and shoddy. They also have an identifiable colour, a reddish glow rather than the lighter copper colour of English plate which is revealed where the silver has worn thin. Finally, if in real doubt there is an acid test which makes it possible to tell the difference between Sheffield plating and Electro-plating. It is advocated by Frederick Bradbury the author of *The History of Old Silver Plate* who advises the application of a spot of nitric acid, slightly diluted with distilled water. When this changes to blue the silver should be of sterling quality. When it stays clear the silver should be pure (as used on electro-plated objects) and the object will have been electro-plated.

Sheffield plate reigned unchallenged until the advent of British plate and the subsequent eclipse of both by electro-plating. However, it was still made on a small scale by one or two firms, including Thomas Bradbury and Sons and James Dixon and Sons, who produced some excellent pieces for the Great Exhibition of 1851 and the International Exhibition of 1862. At the latter they were awarded a medal for "the general excellence of their works in Sheffield plate and electro-plate". The items included tea and coffee services. In 1878, Ridge, Woodcock and Hardy showed their Sheffield plate at the International Exhibition in Paris, but this was probably the last of such exhibits.

CHAPTER 11

Electro-Plate

Electro-plate which can be regarded as the final step in the evolution if mass-produced silver plate, accounted for the final demise of Sheffield and British plate. With its introduction came the surge of seductively priced plated goods which continues to this day.

Nineteenth century electro-plate in general has a less harsh colour than modern electro-plate. It has risen steadily in cost and appears in a constant flow at local antique fairs. The difference in the technique of producing Sheffield plate and electro-plate was that the former was plated in sheet form, the wares being worked up from this, while the latter was placed in the vat after the wares had been made. Manufacturers of Sheffield plate or British plate quite often marked their wares 'plated by fire' when electro-plate was introduced. This indicated that their process was a tried and tested one, compared with the new, as yet untried process.

A patent concerning an entirely new process for coating metals and zinc was first applied for in 1838 by G. R. Elkington and O. W Barratt, and although this did not mention the word 'electricity', it is thought that a single-cell battery was used in what was then an astonishing new process. The use of electricity was remarkable, since, until this innovation, all forms of working metal had relied upon heat from fire. Scientists had been experimenting in electro-metallurgy following Alessandro Volta's invention of an electric battery in 1880. In 1805, Brugnatelli astounded scientists by using electrolysis to coat two silver medals with gold. However, the technique still left much to be desired. Among other technical hazards was the process of getting an even deposit over the entire surface of the object to be treated, and also of bringing this to a permanent form of adherence.

By the second and third decades of the century much progress had been made. Further discoveries in the field of electro-metallurgy resolved many intitial problems and John Wright discovered a way of making the silver plate stick to the surface. In 1840 (nearly 100 years after Thomas Boulsover had discovered that it was possible to fuse silver onto copper) John Wright entered into partnership with Elkington and Company. He prudently contracted to sell them the secrets of this discovery for a sum of money and royalties on all silver deposited on electro-plate, together with all licences granted under the patent.

Although John Wright's discovery was a big step forward, further work was required to perfect it sufficiently for commercial purposes. Other experiments followed and Elkington applied for revised patents. During the course of these a

No. 421

Electro Plate	...	...	...	£0	3 0	each
Silver...	...	...	...	0	10 6	,,

No. 1301

Electro Plate	...	...	...	£0	4 6	each
Silver...	...	...	...	0	14 0	,,

No. 1914

Electro Plate	...	..	...	£0	4 0	each
Silver...	...	...	...	0	11 0	,,

No. 2324

Electro Plate	...	...	...	£0	3 0	each
Silver...	...	...	...	0	12 6	,,

No. 422

Electro Plate	...	...	..	£0	3 0	each
Silver...	...	...	...	0	14 0	,,

process was revealed which contributed to the later making of electrotypes, since it proved that silver or gold might be deposited by electrical means in or on suitable models. During the final years of the 1840's another important process was discovered. This enabled the inclusion of sulphur or carbon compounds to the solution of metals, imparting a more brilliant surface during the process of electro-deposition. During electro-deposition miniscule particles of silver were taken by an electric current from a sheet of pure silver (hung in the vat) and deposited on to the surface of the base metal.

By the time of the Great Exhibition of 1851 the process of plating by electrolysis was well established. Various firms displayed with pride their new electro-plated wares, although the Jury at the Exhibition looked upon these with restraint. Despite this caution, during that decade electro-plating continued unabated and the Jury of the International Exhibition of 1865 declared, "There is no limit to the art which may be employed in the production of plated goods by the new process of electro-deposit, and for articles in daily use it is now found to be quite as durable as the old process . . ."

Electro-plating had thus been given final acknowledgement. Its effects of silver design and production were important. Since, unlike Sheffield plate, there were no technical difficulties in producing precisely the same designs which were made in sterling silver, this now meant that exact replicas could be produced in the inexpensive electro-plate. Manufacturers began to print catalogues showing pages of illustrations of identical wares which could be purchased in either sterling silver or electro-plate.

Electro-plate influenced and accelerated the adoption of mechanical processes in the making of silver objects in general and affected the development of design. Elkingtons were able to encourage and promote the work of artists and designers such as Albert Wilms and L. Morel Ladeuil, while other manufacturers encouraged designers who were producing pieces of silver and electro-plate under the banner of Felix Summerly's Art Manufacturers. This was a group of artists, designers and manufacturers initiated by the eminent designer Henry Cole in 1847 (Henry Cole used the name of Felix Summerly) to produce new ideas and 'to revive the good old practice of connecting the best art with familiar objects in everyday use".

Naturalism, much beloved by the Victorians, was a vital form of decoration on electro-plated wares. The advances in the production of the electrotype now came into their own. Flowers or small creatures (or whatever was desired) could be preserved in a metal coating, enabling designers and modellers to achieve the highest standards in their own interpretations. Perfection in naturalism was considered the ultimate. Electrotypes were favoured for items other than naturalistic forms, however, since they played an important role in sustaining art,

72. *Facing Page: Electro-plated sugar sifter spoons, identical to their sterling silver counterpart in a late nineteenth century catalogue.*

143

including Greek and Roman plate and works of art from the Renaissance period. A room at Marlborough House was allocated specifically for the purpose of making electrotypes of the works of art in the museum.

Towards the final decades of the nineteenth century there came an influx of new ideas and shapes. Christopher Dresser produced designs for electro-plated wares which were far ahead of the times. They were refreshingly simple and functional, with a dismissive attitude towards decoration, quite out of keeping with the general view which favoured a plethora of heavy ornament. His designs for electro-plated wares were made by manufacturers including James Dixon and Sons, Hukin and Heath and Elkingtons. From the late 1870's there was a vogue for Japanese decoration on electro-plated wares as there was on those made in sterling silver, manifesting itself in such ornament as engraved oriental birds and plants. *Art Nouveau,* likewise had its effect on electro-plate, since its fluid lines were conveniently adaptable to most shapes.

The methods of manufacture used in electro-plated wares were generally the same as those used by the silversmith. Some of the early pieces were cast first in German silver or Britannia metal. When the vessel had been hammered up to the required shape, spun or cast, its additional appendages were joined by solder and the completed item was ready to be decorated. This took various forms including hand-engraving; by mechanism such as engine-turned embellishment; and by etching which emulated hand-engraving. Upon completion the piece was placed in the vat for electro-deposition. The wares were carefully checked when they were lifted from the vat, being tapped all over the surface to ensure that the silver plating was firmly affixed. After this they would be burnished by woman – usually – to give them their lustrous appearance.

Although electro-plated wares are not hallmarked (except for those marks which have been ingeniously devised to look like sterling silver hallmarks), there are still ways of dating pieces. One is by a knowledge of style and decoration, related to specific periods, upon which there is much general reading matter. Another is by a system of registry marks which sometimes appears on miscellaneous objects between 1842 and 1883 inclusive. It showed that the object was registered at the British Patent Office, and from it the date of registration can be worked out as well as a guide to the name of the patentee. Items were divided into classes and those for Sheffield plate or electro-plate came into Class I. The mark was formed like a lozenge. Above the top apex of this (facing) is a small circle in which is the class of the goods. Below this circle, inside the lozenge, is the year letter. The left angle of the lozenge contains the month and the right angle the day. The number for the bundle or parcel of goods appears in the bottom angle.

The year letters for 1842 to 1867 are as follows:

73. *Facing page: Waiters in either sterling silver or electro-plate. Early 20th century catalogue.*

No. 5464 E

	ELECTRO PLATE	SILVER
8 inch	£2 2 0	£5 15 0
10 ..	2 18 0	8 12 0
12 ..	3 15 0	12 6 0
14	4 16 0	16 18 0
16 ..	6 4 0	24 2 6

1842 X; 1843 H; 1844 C; 1845 A; 1846 I; 1847 F; 1848 U; 1849 S; 1850 V; 1851 P; 1852 D; 1853 Y; 1854 J; 1855 E; 1856 L; 1857 K; 1858 B; 1859 M; 1860 Z; 1861 R; 1862 O; 1863 G; 1864 N; 1865 W; 1866 Q; 1867 T. Month letters: January C; February G; March W; April H; May E; June M; July I; August R; September D; October B; November K; December A.

From 1868 to 1883, the information was placed differently within the lozenge. The class stayed in a circle above the top apex. The day was inserted beneath this, the number for the bundle or parcel of goods in the left angle and the year in the angle to the right. The month was placed in the angle at the base.

The year letters for 1868 to 1883 are: 1868 X; 1869 H; 1870 C; 1871 A; 1872 I; 1873 F; 1874 U; 1875 S; 1876 V; 1877 P; 1878 D; 1879 Y; 1880 J; 1881 E; 1882 L; 1883 K. The month letters are the same as above except that from March 1 – 6 1878 the letters G and W were used for month and year respectively.

After the year 1883 a serial number replaced the lozenge. It was used for all types of objects. From 1884 to 1895 these were: 1884, 1; 1885, 19754; 1886, 40480; 1887, 64520; 1888, 90483; 1889, 116648; 1890, 141273; 1891, 163767; 1892, 185713; 1893, 205240; 1894, 224720; 1895, 246975.

CHAPTER 12

Silver and its Care

Silver is not difficult to clean, and with the use of certain modern cleaning aids this beautiful metal now requires far less time than our ancestors lavished upon it. When using modern proprietary cleaners for silver, however, read the instructions very carefully, particularly if you are cleaning plated items. Nonetheless proprietary cleaners of repute when used with discretion can prove most satisfactory. In fact, the magnificent silver which glistens in stately homes has often been cleaned by such products.

Always clean silver regularly. This will stop damage resulting from heavy tarnish. Tarnishing is insidious. It is the reaction of silver with certain compounds of sulphur that are in the air or particular foods. Only by cleaning constantly can these be overcome. The compounds integrate with the surface of the silver and form a film of silver sulphide. This results in discolouration of the silver.

Knowing what is most likely to cause discolouration is useful in the care of silver. Some sources can be avoided. Others, alas, are present most of the time. They include gases from the burning of oil, petrol, coal, gas and logs. If you use a coal, log or gas fire, therefore, you are at an immediate disadvantage, as you are if you live in a town where the air is polluted.

Among the foods which will cause discolouration are eggs, fish, peas, vinegar and lemon juice. The worst culprit is salt. Salt will corrode all silver. Silver salt cellars should, therefore, always be emptied and cleaned after use. This also applies to salt spoons. Wash at once and with extreme thoroughness. When salt cellars have glass liners, although these protect the silver to a certain degree, they are by no means the ultimate preventative to corrosion. Salt can slip between the liner and the silver case. It is important, therefore, to empty the salt from the cellar, remove the glass liner and to wash it at the same time as the silver cellar. Even a gilt-lined cellar may have pitfalls, for once the gilt is worn the salt can reach the silver beneath and cause corrosion.

When drying silver after washing, apply a circular movement. This technique should also be used when cleaning and polishing. Avoid cleaning larger pieces of silver on a hard surface (like a table top). If you can, hold such pieces against the body, or if this is not possible, place them on an old cushion.

If you do not wish to polish your silver regularly with one of the proprietary silver cloths, a regular washing in warm or hot soapy water, or a little mild detergent, will keep the silver clean if it has not come into contact with any of the sources which ultimate lead to corrosion. The best way to find out whether a mere washing will suffice is to try the method for a short time before resorting to cleaners. Remember, though, that since most water contains chlorine, which discolours silver, never leave silver wet. Always dry immediately. Should silver become badly corroded it is best left in the hands of a jeweller for a thorough cleaning. When this is not too extreme, jeweller's rouge is sometimes effective. Do not use a brush or anything which is hard or harsh. Intricate ornament may be cleaned with ammonia and French chalk. Apply gently and rub carefully with a soft cloth. For the removal of verdigris, black spot and lacquer from silver or silver gilt, it is again better to leave the piece in the hands of an expert.

Silver-Gilt

Treat silver-gilt very gently when cleaning. Gilt is delicate. Paul de Lamerie, the great Huguenot silversmith, had straightforward advice on the matter, and it applies as much today as it did in the eighteenth century. "Clean it now and then with only warm water and soap with a sponge, and then wash it with clean water, and dry it very well with a soft Linnen Cloth and keep it in a dry place for the damp will spoil it". He might have added, avoid all abrasives and never use a brush.

Gold

Gold is very much softer than silver. Treat it carefully. Wash it in a weak solution of liquid ammonia or gentle detergent. Polish with care using a soft cloth.

Storing

This is an area where people unwittingly encounter problems, since they often wrap silver or silver-gilt in the first piece of discarded paper or cloth that comes to hand. This may prove dangerous. Do not use newspaper, brown paper or blankets. Always use a sulphur-free paper or one that contains very little sulphur. Tissue paper is ideal. You can also buy a specially treated sulphur-free paper from many good jewellers. Never use rubber bands to secure the paper because rubber is rich in sulphur.

Products for Cleaning

There are several proprietary products available for the cleaning of silver. Read what the label says with care before applying. Reputable firms usually have technical staff trained to assist and to answer queries from customers with problems concerning their silver.

The products available include the following:

A polish with a long term ingredient. This forms an invisible chemical barrier on the surface of the metal which inhibits tarnish. Silver therefore stays cleaner for a longer period.

A long term silver foam which is particularly useful for pieces of silver with intricate decoration, embossing or repoussé work. The foam is applied with a soft sponge which is usually provided and the foam finds its way into the crevices and corners which are difficult to clean by ordinary methods. The foam is rinsed off and the silver dried thoroughly with a soft cloth.

A liquid silver dip which is intended for certain types of cutlery. Having ascertained that it is appropriate for the cutlery, this is then placed in the dip briefly to remove tarnish. The cutlery is removed, given a thorough rinsing, dried and polished.

A long term silver cloth which is impregnated with a special ingredient. This is beneficial for regular polishing, once the silver has been brought up to a good standard of cleanliness.

Insurance and Theft

If you display your silver keep it well away from windows so that it cannot be easily seen by intruders from the outside of the house.

It is worth taking the trouble to photograph items of which you are particularly fond, or which are valuable. Should you be burgled such photographs may assist the police in their recovery.

Insurance is important. Items should first be valued so that they can be insured for the correct amount. Certain dealers will value silver for you. They work on a fixed rate which is a percentage of the value of the silver. Once this is done, remember that antiques usually appreciate rather than depreciate. You must therefore make sure that the insurance company is aware of the fact that the item is an antique so that the company can quote you the appropriate premium.

Glossary

Acanthus Plant with attractive, prickly leaves, applied in stylized form as embellishment on Corinthian capitals and classical architecture, from which the derivative adorns silver. Particularly fashionable during the neo-classical period.

Alloy A combination of base and precious metals. Also a combination of ordinary metals.

Anthemion A motif similar to the flower of the honeysuckle.

Art Nouveau A style derived from a combination of Japanese and medieval ideas.

Baluster An ornate shape found in candlesticks, stems and other objects. Slender above and bulging below.

Beading Small bulbous shapes like 'beads', used as a decorative border or in conjunction with other ornament.

Bombé A rotund, prominent shape with a low waist.

Bright-cutting A form of engraving with a faceted effect.

Britannia metal An alloy with a silver colour incorporating tin, antimony and copper.

Britannia standard The higher standard of silver, marked with the figure of Britannia, with 958 parts of pure silver per thousand.

Cartouche A decorative frame in which inscriptions, initials, coats-of-arms, etc. are engraved.

Casting A technique for making components and decorative motifs, etc. A mould of the required shape is made, from which an impression is taken in two halves, clamped together and the molten silver is poured into this.

Chasing Decoration on the surface of the metal with hammer and punches, by which no metal is removed.

Chinoiseries Ornament with Chinese-inspired ideas, primitively used in the later years of the seventeenth century, but with sophistication during the rococo period and thereafter. Later described as 'being in the Chinese style'.

Cut-card work Decorative motifs, cut from a separate sheet of silver and soldered onto the object. Much beloved by Huguenot craftsmen.

Die-stamping The stamping out of items from silver by means of steel dies.

Electro-plating The application by electrolysis of a coating of silver to objects made of a base metal.

Electrotyping A process for making identical copies of existing items.

Embossing A method of producing raised decoration on the surface, which is worked from the back with hammer and punches.

Engraving Cutting decorative lines into the surface of the metal with a sharp tool which removes the metal.

151

Festoons   Garlands of decorative fruit, flowers, etc. hanging in a balanced curve.
Finial   Ornament surmounting the top or end of an object.
Flat chasing   Low relief surface decoration, without removing the metal.
Fluting   Half-round parallel channels, which might be vertical, oblique or curved.
Gadrooning   Inverted fluting, generally applied to edging.
German silver   A white metal alloy.
Key pattern   A repetitive pattern consisting of straight lines at right angles.
Knop   A decorative protuberance on the end of stem.
Ogee   A shape which shows in section a double continuous curve, concave below passing into convex above.
Ovolo   A half-round or curved convex moulding used as a repeat border.
Patera   Circular classical ornament, based on the saucer used in sacrificial libations.
Pyriform   Pear-shaped.
Reeding   A convex decoration consisting of narrow parallel ridges.
Repoussé   Embossing worked from the back of the metal, with decorative effects.
Scorper   A small chisel for engraving.
Sheffield plate   Copper to which silver has been fused.
Silver-gilt   Silver to which a fine layer of gold has been applied.
Soldering   A technique used to join two or more pieces of silver by employing an alloy that melts at a lower temperature than the silver.
Spinning   A method of producing hollow vessels on a spinning lathe. A circle of silver is spun around a hard-wood head until the required shape is formed.
Strapwork   Decorative lengths of straight or curved strapping.
Swag   A decoration consisting of festoons of draped cloth.
Volute   A decorative scroll

Bibliography

Frederick Bradbury, Bradbury's Book of Hallmarks (J. W. Northend Ltd.)

Frederick Bradbury, A History of Old Sheffield Plate (Macmillan)

Michael Clayton, The Collector's Dictionary of the Silver and Gold of Great Britain and North America (Country Life)

C. Willett Cunnington and Phillis Cunnington, A Handbook of English Costume in the 17th Century (Faber and Faber)

Elizabeth de Castres, A Collector's Guide to Tea Silver 1670–1900 (Muller)

Elizabeth de Castres, A Guide to Collecting Silver (Queen Anne Press)

Elizabeth de Castres, The Observer's Book of Silver (Warne)

Eric Delieb, Investing in Silver (Barrie and Jenkins)

Eric Delieb, Silver Boxes (Barrie and Jenkins)

J. F. Hayward, Huguenot Silver in England 1688–1727 (Faber and Faber)

G. Bernard Huges, Antique Sheffield Plate (Batsford)

Bernard and Therle Hughes, Three Centuries of English Domestic Silver 1500–1820 (Lutterworth)

Norman M. Penzer, The Book of the Wine Label (White Lion Publishers)

Gerald Taylor, Silver (Penguin)

Patricia Wardle, Victorian Silver and Silver-plate (Barrie and Jenkins)

Booklets: Touching Gold and Silver, 500 years of Hallmarks
(The Goldsmiths' Company)

The Colman Collection of Silver Mustard Pots
(Colman Foods Ltd.)

Catalogue: Matthew Boulton and the Toymakers – Silver from the Birmingham Assay Office. (An exhibition held at Goldsmiths' Hall, Foster Lane, London)

Index